WHAT DOES YOUR DAD DO ?

RUCHA PANTOJI

Contents

Contents

Also By Rucha Pantoji

Find More On: www.ruchapantoji.com

CHAPTER ONE

PROLOGUE

"Thank you all for being here to celebrate my Dad's 34 years of glorious work life." I was standing on a podium, holding a mic, giving a speech at my Dad's retirement ceremony. A farewell to his 34 years of a job at Central Railways India. A celebration of his marvelous achievements. The hall was filled with hundreds of people who all wanted my Dad to stay at work a little longer. There was a different kind of energy in that hall, an energy of inspiration.

The farewell party was simple. We had booked the hall at the Railway Library building. Half section of the building was allocated to the library and the other half was divided into the party hall and lunch area.

My Dad had invited his entire department, including Daund and all other towns under the Solapur Section of Central Railways. The party hall was too small to allocate so many people. Eventually, we decided to set up the stage and the venue on the cricket ground outside the library. The stage was decorated with flowers and lights. A long table and a few chairs were arranged for the committee to sit along with my father. A long red carpet from the entrance of the venue to the stage was adding more beauty to the ceremony. And, a poster behind the stage was displaying in big bold letters: 'Farewell Party for Chief Signal Inspector Mr. Anand Pantoji.' It was a simple yet beautiful decoration.

Dad was sitting on a middle chair behind the table with mom sitting beside him with pride. The rest of the chairs were occupied by higher authority officers working in the same section as my father. His colleagues were greeting him with gifts and bouquets on the stage. Some of his friends shared their experiences of working with him. Some joyful memories brought laughter and some heart-touching stories brought tears to his eyes. People really admired my father and his work.

Dad insisted I give a final speech and I was more than happy to share our story on the stage. When I stepped down the stage after my speech and looked around the hall, a thought came into my mind. My Dad had a remarkable career worth bragging about by his kids. I have seen him work under pressure, pick up his coat, and ride on a bicycle to the emergency failures in the railway signaling department in the middle of the night. Skipping lunch and sometimes dinner too. Sleeping in the wide-open waiting area at the station, even on cold days. Walking through railway tracks for inspections, spending a considerable amount of his married life alone living in employee quarters where a snake could crawl over your body or a lizard could fall from the roof in your plate, he adjusted in all situations for the sake of work and never complained about his sleepless nights. He loved his job. And he wanted his wife and daughters to have a comfortable life. He didn't care about anything else.

That day I saw tears in my Dad's eyes as he was talking about his life at Central Railways. And I decided to share how difficult, adventurous, and fun the life of a dedicated railway employee can be. People who love their work more than anything, even more than themselves, are rare species. My Dad inspired me to keep going no matter how difficult things can get at times. I always wonder, if I was in his place, I would have never been able to do what he did in his life. His love and dedication to work are inspiring and worth sharing.

I am Rucha Pantoji, and this is my Dad's story.

CHAPTER TWO

WHAT DOES YOUR DAD DO?

I grew up in Daund, a peaceful town near Pune, considerably away from the noisy chaos yet connected to major cities via trains. Being a junction, Daund welcomes trains from almost everywhere.

My school was right next to Daund railway station and closer to my Dad's office. Dad used to drop me at school on his way to work. I used to enjoy sitting in the backseat of his cycle. We would hear trains passing by blowing a whistle, on our way to school.

When I was a kid, I was annoyingly talkative. People would beg my Mom to keep my mouth shut. But some people thought I was cute. So they would ask me questions about myself or my school just to hear my response. I would answer every question correctly with factual details, except one question- what does your Dad do?

I could only answer "he works for railways" but wasn't sure what exactly he does. Then people would ask me a follow-up question, "Does he drives trains?" I would picture him driving the train, holding the steering (because that's how 5-year-old me thought the train works). My usual response would be, "He goes to the railway station every day. I don't think he drives the train though."

One day, I thought maybe I should ask my Dad what exactly his job is. I sat in the front yard of our house, holding a pencil and paper in hand, and waited for him to return from the office. As soon as I saw his cycle from far away, I was ready to ask him lots of questions.

"Hey little one," he greeted me with a smile and saw a big question mark on my face. "Do you need something?"

"Dad," I waited till he sat beside me on a bench in our front yard and asked, "what is your job?"

"What?" He didn't see that coming. The look on his face was as confused as I was about his job.

"I mean, I know you work for railways, but what exactly do you do?"

He laughed and looked into my curious eyes. "Little one, your Dad works at the Signaling and Telecommunication Department."

"What is that?" I asked as I couldn't understand a word he said. Just then, Mom came out with a tray of tea and some snacks. "Explain her in simple words, she is just 5," she chuckled and placed the tray in between us, and offered me some cookies. I took a mouth full of bite and looked at Dad's confused face again. He took a sip of the hot ginger tea and finally came up with the simple answer to my question, "Have you seen green, yellow, and red light signals on the street?"

"Yeah, you go when it's green and stop when it's red," I proudly smiled ear to ear and looked at him to see his response.

"Just like that, railways have signals too. I work to make sure those signals work properly so that every train gets a free way to drive away."

"So you press buttons to turn on red lights and that's why the train stops at the station?"

Dad looked at my Mom who was hiding her laughter. "Not really. But right now you don't have to understand everything. If anybody asks where your Dad works, you can answer- he is a Signaling Engineer at Railways."

I handed him the paper and the pencil, "Dad, do you mind writing it down for me?" And so he did. I learned those words and decided to inform my friends at school that my Dad does not drive the train, he switches on the signal lights.

Little me couldn't understand anything beyond picturing my Dad switching on/off the signal lights. I thought that's what proper working of signal meant. But that was literally 0.99% of my Dad's job. He had to check all the tracks are intact and secure for a train to pass by, all the signals are working as expected, the relay room controlling the signals is error-free, and all the railway gates protecting residential areas are fully functional. He was handling the most important and stressful job, making sure no train derails or collapses with another train or any other thing on the route. He was ensuring the safety of people traveling by trains.

My Dad's father, his 2 uncles, and even my Mom's father worked in central railways. Grandpa had a similar job as my father. Half of my family spent their lives serving Central Indian railways. So I would always wonder if I will have to join my Dad's stream of work when I get older. Might as well be prepared, I thought when I asked him about his work.

Every person has to go through different kinds of struggles at work and in life in general. Every job profile comes with huge responsibility and stress. But it's in the person's hands to enjoy that work stress with dedication.

My Dad had nailed the art of loving his job. So, to the people who asked 5-year-old me- what does your dad do? The fun stories in this book are my answers to the question.

CHAPTER THREE

GRANDPA'S ADVICE

Indian Railways have a total of 18 zones that are further subdivided into divisions and led by the Divisional Railway Manager (DRM). My father and grandfather both worked in the Solapur division of central railways.

During the 50s, Indian railways did not have a touch of technology. Most of the tasks were manual. My grandfather joined the department of Signalling and Telecommunication (S&T) at Daund Taluka. He had to travel through all the stations between Daund-Solapur and Wadi in Karnataka state. At that time, there were no electric poles of signals. A man would show a green/yellow/red kerosene lantern during the night hours or a flag during the day. However, some of the sections were on the way to electrifying the stations and installing mechanical signal poles.

Grandpa would have to work for 20 hours a day. Sometimes he would travel through all the stations for signal inspection and return home after 8 days without prior notice to my grandmother. But she knew what she was marrying into.

Every day, she would prepare a lunch box for Grandpa and send one of her children to the station. Either my Dad or uncle would then hand over the tiffin box to the guard of the train going to the station where Grandpa was working. Grandma would send a meal for 4 to 5 people, so everyone working day and night with Grandpa would get homemade food.

At that time my Dad and his 3 siblings- Anupam, Aruna, and Anil, were little kids. They were spending their days studying and playing. One day, Grandpa came home worried and stressed. His pale face was clearly showing that something was bothering him. His children were playing in the front yard of the railway quarter. Usually, Grandpa would greet his kids with a big smile and join them in the game. That day he just went inside and did not speak for hours. Grandma kept asking questions, which were not answered for a long time. Grandpa was laying on the bed quietly until dinner was ready.

"Would you please tell me what happened at the work?" Grandma asked again and again during dinner. Finally, Grandpa broke down and told everything. What had happened at work wasn't directly Grandpa's fault, but his department had to take responsibility for the incident of two trains almost colliding with each other. Due to the failure of interlocking at one of the ends of the track, a military train changed the route to the loop line (alongside the platform) where already a passenger train was arriving. Thankfully, the cabin man at the other end signaled the alert to the military train driver and he stopped the train at around 200 meters from the other train. A little bit of delay might have caused a terrible accident. There were hundreds of people traveling by those two trains including military officers, families, and little kids.

Grandpa's eyes filled with tears when he was talking about the incident. "Don't worry. Everything will be alright," Grandma tried to comfort him. Both of them knew what was coming his way. Grandpa was well aware that he could get suspended.

"My team solved the failure immediately after that. But there will be an inquiry and investigation of the incident since it was the S&T department's responsibility, which means I am responsible for it. There will be some consequences," Grandpa said and looked at his children who were listening to all this in horror. He immediately wiped his tears and hugged his kids assuring them that there is nothing to worry about, at least not for them.

"Dad, don't worry. Everybody knows how sincerely you work," assured my father to his father.

"Anand, come here son. Kids... you all come here," Grandpa held all his children closer, "I know you all are too young for this. But whatever job you get in the future, always keep your eyes, ears, and brain alert. No matter what, don't blindly trust anything or anyone. Okay? Stay alert all the time."

"Okay, Dad," the children replied. My Dad did not understand the importance of Grandpa's advice at that time. But he still remembers those words.

After the inquiry of the incident, Grandpa was transferred to Bhusawal in the Jalgaon district of Maharashtra. Dad and his siblings were sad to leave Daund, their school, and their beloved friends behind. Leaving home behind. But nobody complained about it.

Grandma packed all the stuff and bid goodbye to her friends in the neighbourhood who had helped her a lot during her pregnancy. She promised to write letters to them. They all traveled by train to Bhusawal. Grandpa did not speak much during the journey. But aunt Aruna, his sweet little daughter made him smile throughout the journey.

CHAPTER FOUR

Adjusting to the New Town

"Breakfast is ready," Grandma announced from the kitchen to call her children. She had built the cooking chulha (traditional Indian gas fire/stove) out of some bricks and mud in the kitchen of the new railway quarter. The quarter was different, a little smaller than the one from Daund. But she managed to set up her kitchen within a few hours. Her children helped her unpack the bags while Grandpa was out at work to set up his new office and meet his colleagues.

Dad and his siblings took a seat on the kitchen floor around their mother. She had turned the leftover *Chapatis* (Rotis) from the last night into the delicious breakfast dish that she served on four plates. Kids peacefully finished their breakfast and started unpacking the rest of the things, including their school books.

As soon as Grandpa came back home in the afternoon, he took all the kids to enroll them in a new school. The school was 6 miles from the railway quarter, unlike the school in Daund which was closer to home. Dad, uncle Anupam, and uncle Anil did not care much about the distance. But Aunt Aruna frowned at Grandpa.

Grandpa sat on his knees, held his daughter closer to him, and said, "You will make new friends here as well. And your brothers will be here too. They will look after you if you need anything," Grandpa looked at his three sons and narrowed his eyes, "right boys?" The boys replied in harmony, "Right".

The school building was single-storied, with a big playground widespread in front of it. Dad took a moment to scan the new school and immediately started missing his old school and the playground. He and his friends had spent countless hours playing cricket. Part of him wanted to run back to his old school. Instead, he decided to make new friends in the new school and entered the admission office along with his siblings. The school principal and a senior teacher asked a few questions to all four of them before enrolling them in the class.

On the way home, Grandpa got an ice cream bar for his children to congratulate them. Soon, my Dad started going to the new school with his siblings. They did not have a bicycle or public transport to go to school. They would all walk 6 miles to reach school and 6 miles back home. Grandma would wake up at 5 in the morning to prepare lunch boxes. Kids would leave the home an hour prior to school time to reach on time. In the evening, they would return home tired, soaking in sweat, and hungry. Bhusawal's heat was unbearable to them.

Grandma couldn't see her children tired and miserable. She had seen neighbourhood children going to school on their bicycles. As soon as Grandpa returned from the office, Grandma decided to propose the idea of purchasing at least 2 cycles for her children.

"Dad... Anil, and I will share one cycle. Brother Anupam will take Aruna with him on one cycle. We don't want separate cycles for all of us," my Dad, with an encouraging smile from Grandma, requested politely to his father.

"I will try to arrange the cycles as soon as possible," assured Grandpa. Till then, all kids walked to the school without asking another question. They knew that their father would fulfill the promise. And as assured, Grandpa arranged two second-hand cycles within a week. He polished, oiled, repaired broken parts, and painted the cycles himself. To surprise his children, Grandpa hid the cycles in the backyard.

"Mother, we are home," Dad and his siblings threw their school bags into the porch. Grandma had a rule, entering a home without washing up was not allowed. There was a small water tap installed near the backdoor, specifically to wash up. All the kids ran to the backyard to get fresh.

Grandpa was sitting in a chair, reading the newspaper with a cup of tea. He knew kids will come straight to the backyard after school. He waited to give them a surprise. "Dad, what's under that cover?" asked my father to his father. Grandpa stood up from his seat, neatly folding the newspaper, "Come on here kids," he gestured and walked to the hidden treasure he had arranged for his kids. All four children stood in one line, curious to know what was hidden under the cover.

Grandpa uncovered the gift slowly. As soon as two shiny cycles appeared beneath the cover, children started screaming and dancing in happiness.

Dad grabbed one of the cycles and uncle Anupam gestured for aunt Aruna to sit in the backseat of the other cycle. Kids rode the cycles through the neighbourhood, woohooing and screaming in happiness. Those cycles were no less than Aladdin's carpet to them.

Grandpa saw the kids returning home with their new cycles and a few friends from the neighbourhood. He smiled in satisfaction as he saw his children adjusting to the new town.

CHAPTER FIVE

DISCIPLINE

Bhusawal was a city of warm summer, much warmer than Daund. Complaining about the heat was a regular topic of conversation. Water problems, electricity problems, and of course, dealing with children were Grandma's favorite topics in her ladies' group. Soon, my Dad, uncles, and aunt made a lot of friends in school and in the neighbourhood. A bunch of kids started showing up at Grandpa's house unannounced. Grandma would get annoyed by their noise and mess. But she would allow them to play in the front yard.

They all would meet at the end of the railway quarter lane and go to school together. After school, aunt Aruna used to return home immediately. Sincere-student inside her didn't allow her to waste much time, she preferred completing her homework on time. Besides, Grandma never allowed her to stay out long. But Dad and my uncles were naughty kids. They would roam around the town, then go to the railway playground where kids of railway employees had free access to sports equipment. Dad and his friends would play cricket until someone from the neighbourhood came searching and yelling at all of them, "are you guys ever planning to return home or want to live here?" Then everyone would run straight home.

"Why do they get to play this long?" aunt Aruna would complain once in a while. But she was a studious kid and completing homework was more important to her. She was the smartest of all the siblings and Grandpa was proud of his daughter. He wanted her to get as much education as she wanted, get a good job, and settle in life. So he would never let her engage in house chores for more than an hour.

Dad, on the other hand, hated studies. He would study when the exams were right around the corner of the month, secure passing marks and that was all, he thought, was sufficient. When the results came, Dad would hide his mark sheet. But the school asked for the father's signature on the mark sheet. Dad knew, if he let Grandpa sign the sheet, Grandpa would be mad at him for not getting good marks. To avoid all the scolding, Dad and uncle Anupam came up with a solution. They would ask for Grandpa's sign on the mark sheet whenever he was about to leave for the office, thinking he wouldn't notice the scores in a rush. The trick worked.

One day, Grandpa was cleaning all the bookshelves and cupboards to throw unnecessary stuff away. He came across mark sheets of his kids and decided to keep them in separate folders. He saw aunt Aruna's mark sheets and his chest filled with pride. Separating all her scorecards in a folder, he began sorting mark sheets of his boys.

Dad and my uncles, who all were enjoying their time at the cricket ground, did not even know what was waiting for them back home. Grandpa saw all the mark sheets that he had signed without paying attention to the grades. He was pissed.

When all three of his sons returned home from the playground, Grandpa was so mad that he took the keys to both bicycles from them and glared at them saying, "You will not have the cycle until you complete today's homework. And from tomorrow, I will be checking all of your homework sharp at 6 in the morning. So keep your notebooks ready before going to bed. Clear?"

The boys nodded and sat next to aunt Aruna to complete the homework. Aunt Aruna giggled to her brothers getting a lecture from their father. That day, Dad realized how much Grandpa cared about discipline. From the next day, Grandpa began checking the homework of all his kids carefully, making sure they are not fooling him.

When Dad and Grandpa told me the story of 'hiding mark sheets', they were both laughing. I could see a lot of memories rewinding in their hearts. Dad always said, Grandpa taught him discipline, which further turned his work-life into a big success.

CHAPTER SIX

DAYDREAMING

"Kids, let's go. The train will be here in 5 minutes," Grandpa called his children while gathering the luggage. Every summer holiday, my Dad and his siblings would go to spend time with their grandparents in Solapur city. Grandpa's parents, brothers, sisters and their children were all staying in the small railway quarter in the neighbourhood next to Solapur railway station. Grandpa would drop his children at his parents, spend a day with his brothers, and return to duty.

Dad used to have an amazing time in Solapur. All the cousins together had a special bond with each other. Playing all day long and returning home to delicious food cooked by their Grandmother was indeed a delight. That place, as my Dad says, was peaceful. The neighbourhood had around 10 railway quarters, each with only 2 rooms and one kitchen. Back then, those quarters did not have a washroom attached. There was one common washroom a mile away from the quarters. It had four bathrooms. Nobody cared about hygiene. Not that it wasn't clean, but the entire neighbourhood had access to those bathrooms.

Waking up early in the morning to make a queue in front of the bathroom was a big task. People used to fight over their turn. And if, someone had a *nature's call emergency'*, then it would get more interesting. Dad says it was fun watching those fights.

Women fighting around the water tanker to fill the containers with fresh drinking water was another topic of entertainment. My great-grandmother used to fill 5 containers of drinking water from the tanker early in the morning and carry them home all by herself. She never had to fight as she was punctual and rather humble. Whenever my Dad and uncles were staying with her, they used to help her with house chores.

There was a big ground in front of the quarters where Dad, his siblings, and the kids from the neighbourhood would spend the entire summer playing cricket.

One of Grandpa's brothers, Aravind Pantoji, was working in the Carriage and Wagon department. And the other one, Vasant Pantoji, was the manager of court cases of railway departments.

One day, Dad's uncle Aravind called him before leaving for work. "Come on Anand, I will show you around my office." Dad jumped at the opportunity as going to the railway office and sneaking at various departments to see how they work was one of his hobbies. The Carriage and Wagon department was something he had never seen before.

When they reached the office, Dad saw tons of journals, registers, and piles of papers on the desk of his uncle. Uncle Aravind grabbed a chair for his nephew and took a seat behind his desk. Dad looked around the room full of shelves. Some old models of train engines, medals, trophies won by the department, and some photo frames were adding beauty to those shelves. Uncle Aravind let the curious boy sink into the situation and said, "Managing the servicing of carriages needs good management and tally skills, son."

Dad shifted his focus to his uncle. "Look here," his uncle opened a recent record in the journal, "see these big numbers? Those are just for this week's servicing, washing, materials, and goods. I make sure all the train carriages are well-serviced and damage-free. Making an entry of every task in this register is important to review and tally the work schedule. Your father manages the servicing of tracks and signals, I make sure the trains themselves are well-serviced."

Dad tried to understand the journal and curiously looked at his uncle who further explained to him, "Always remember, Anand, that numbers never lie. Paying attention to the numbers will keep your work thorough, safe, and perfectly scheduled. You have to make sure nothing unethical is happening. Being the head of the office makes you responsible for the actions happening in your department."

Dad carefully listened to what his uncle was trying to explain to him. To survive in a crucial job, under departmental politics; without compromising ethics could be tough. Dad spent an hour with his uncle, gaining lessons on management skills. It fascinated him. His dreams to become an officer at the railways grew bigger that day. While returning home from the station, Dad saw an old steam engine showcased outside the Solapur station. He had seen it so many times. But that day, looking at that shiny steam engine enlightened his dreams.

After that, whenever Dad went to Solapur in the summer holidays, he would go to his uncle's office to help him, to learn new lessons, and to tally numbers. His mathematics skills drastically improved, which made

Grandpa happier than ever. Dad was growing from a naughty careless kid to a responsible man. Whenever he went to the offices of Grandpa or his uncles, he felt the urge to work for the railways.

He had understood what daydreaming feels like.

CHAPTER SEVEN

THE MAN OF HONESTY

Today, Indian railways have evolved and improved with technology and automation. But in the 70s, it was different, mostly manual, yet effective to manage the whole schedule of trains running in central railways. Today, a single button on the panel can set the tracks, create the rail-line, and alert the signals in the whole area. But back then, the Neale's Token system was the backbone of train schedules and communication.

The Station Master and the two cabin men at the opposite ends of the track used to manage the process of safe passage of trains. The two cabins had levers (mechanical switches that looked like rifles but were actually used to create the track crossings/switches) associated with the tracks. The tracks are of two types, the mainline and the loop line. The Loop line is always adjacent to the platform. The mainline runs between the loop lines. If the train has a halt at the station, it always arrives on the loop line otherwise pass by the mainline.

To set the appropriate track, cabin men from both ends of the track pull the matching levers associated with the crossing and create a line for the train. The Neale's token machine resides in the station master's office. By pulling the nob on the machine, the Station Master takes out a ball token which he exchanges with the driver of the train arriving at the loop line. The token of the driver should have the matching code to confirm the clear line ahead and secure the path. After taking the token from the driver and handing him the new token, the station master makes the entry of the train in the register. The token machine gets locked until the train goes beyond the specific radius. Some sections used to have the ball token system while some had a tablet token system. In both systems, the driver and the station master should have identical tokens with matching codes.

Four people, doing different jobs, would effectively communicate with each other. And that was the scenario in the 70s when there was no automation yet the whole management was fascinating.

Mom's father, my Nanna, was a punctual, smart, professional, and ethical man. He was Station Master at Madha, near Solapur district. During his work life, he hardly took a day off, was never late to work, and honestly worked for the railways. Even though his department was to manage a railway station, he was really good at legal work and railway court cases-related paperwork as well.

His daily routine was to wake up early, have breakfast with his three children, go to work, and do the routine procedure of Neale's token by communicating with cabin men to set routes for the trains.

One day, Nanna left the railway quarter at a regular time and went to duty. He was working peacefully in silence as no train was due for another hour. One empty passenger train was waiting at the platform, the train had the halt at Madha for another 10 minutes. He performed his tasks regarding the passenger train and was busy doing paperwork when the telephone on his desk rang, almost screeching and breaking the silence.

He picked up the phone and said, "You have reached Madha station, this is Station Master Nanjkar."

"Sir, we have a big problem," said the cabin man.

"Why? What happened?" Nanna asked, pausing the work he was doing.

"A goods train has entered the loop line even though the signal wasn't green."

"What?" Nanna panicked. A passenger train was already waiting on the platform. He had to stop the goods train. He asked the cabin man with fear humming down his body, "How is it possible?"

The cabin man had no answers and neither did Nanna. The goods train wasn't supposed to be there in the first place. But now it was running towards the empty passenger train peacefully standing by the platform. The passenger train had no idea what was coming towards it.

Nanna thought for a moment and ran towards the engine of the passenger train. He called the driver, "You need to move the train backward and get to the mainline."

"What? How...erm...why?"

"Do it quick. The goods train is approaching towards you," Nanna explained in a rush and asked the driver to try his best to move the train.

Moving the train is never as easy as reversing a car or a bus. It had to be taken back to the crossing and then to the mainline. This wasn't the optimal solution but was the only way to stop both trains from colliding. The driver of the passenger train started backing off the train. He tried to make it just a few meters away from the crossing when he knew it was impossible to stop the accident. The goods train was approaching fast, almost at the edge of collision when the driver of the passenger train jumped off the engine and ran to save his life. Thankfully the train did not have any passengers on board.

As soon as the driver rushed towards the side of the yard, the two trains bumped into each other face to face. The scene in front of the Madha railway station was horrifying. The carriages of both trains were scattered in the yard, breaking the water pipes. Some carriages even dented and broke the platform. The driver of the passenger train was alert enough to save his life. But the driver of the goods train died in the accident.

"How did this all happen?" Nanna asked the cabin men who were now on the accident scene. After evaluating every little detail, Nanna understood that the goods train wasn't supposed to enter the Madha station as there was no green signal. And the crossing-switch created for the passenger train to get on a loop line was supposed to go back to the mainline.

"Sir, the passenger train was going to leave soon anyway. We kept the switch to the loop line to let the train drive away. But this goods train came out of nowhere," a cabin man who was sweating in panic was trying to understand what could have been done. The system back then was strong enough to avoid any such glitches. To open the loop-line alongside the platform for the train or to create a crossing, both the cabin men from the opposite ends of the track pull the lever associated with that crossing. The station master confirms the arrangement of levers to make sure the accurate crossing has been set. And, while the crossing is still active, the signal never goes green for that particular track. That day, the driver of the goods train should not have continued on the same track as the signal wasn't green and the cabin men should have closed the crossing on time. It was a collective glitch. But the worst had happened already and there was no way to undo it.

Nanna had to see the terrible train accident in front of him. His heart started pounding faster, sweat dripping from his forehead to his eyes making them burn. The whole yard was a mess, carriages were all over the tracks. Nanna had to cancel or halt the upcoming trains. The entire Solapur division got the news of this horrible incident.

Nanna sat down on his chair, panicked and helpless. He knew there will be an investigation, and people will point fingers at him. Even though this was not his fault, he was in charge of the station at the time of the incident. He had to take responsibility.

The Commissioner of Railway safety along with his team arrived at the accident spot. The life of a driver of the goods train had been compromised.

After investigating the accident scene, the Commissioner came to Nanna's cabin, "A fast-approaching goods train collided with the standing passenger train," the commissioner began the interrogation. "Mr. Nanjkar, you were in charge of the station at the time of the incident, is that correct?"

"Yes," replied my Nanna.

"What was the status of the track lines?" the officer asked.

Nanna explained everything he could about the accident with a huge disappointment spread over his face. The interrogation went on for 3 hours. My Nanna and a few other employees were suspended from work for 6 months. The news of the incident traveled through the whole Solapur division at a speed of a fast express train. People started creating all kinds of theories about it. Some blamed the driver and said he was not in his senses. Some blamed the cabin man, and of course, my Nanna. Nanna did not leave the house for a week.

Whenever my Nanni (Mom's mother) went to the market, people would circle around her to get inside information about the accident. She tried to avoid it. But as it all got overwhelming, she stopped going out too. It was my Mom, who was just 15, and her two little siblings, Avinash and Asha, who had to step out of the house for school and had to face similar questioning by people.

Two weeks after the incident, Mom and her siblings were in the school having a completely normal day when a professor approached my Mom and asked, "why are you still in school? You should be at home. Your mother needs you." My mother could not understand the context. She just nodded to the professor's question. During the lunch break, Mom and her siblings met to share the lunch box at their regular spot.

"You know," said aunt Asha to her sister, "something really weird happened with me today."

"What?"

"Professor asked why I am still in school and that our Mom needs us. Something unclear, but he seemed serious."

"He asked me the exact same question," said uncle Avi. A friend of my Mom's approached them and said, "Anju, I think you all should go home."

"Why? What's happening?" Mom asked wondering why everyone was trying to send them home.

"Don't you know?"

"Know what?"

"Your father committed suicide. After the train incident...you know. People are saying it was his fault so he hung himself."

"What? When?" Mom's eyes soon filled with tears as she held both of her siblings together. Quickly, all three of them packed their bags and hurried home. Their school was in the main town, far away from the railway area. It took them almost an hour to walk home as there was no public transport nor they had cycles. As soon as they reached home, all three children rushed through the main door.

They had imagined all kinds of horrible stuff on their way back home. But when they entered the home, it was quiet. Nothing unusual. They heard Nanni doing laundry as they ran to the backyard and saw Nanna reading the newspaper. He was perfectly fit and very much alive.

"What are you doing at home? Did your classes end early today?" Nanni asked her three children.

"No," Mom replied, still looking at Nanna. "They sent us home."

"Why?" Nanni asked, still doing her laundry.

Aunt Asha started crying and Mom explained everything that happened at the school. She had tears rolling down her cheeks. Nanna and Nanni were shocked. People were creating rumors about the accident, but this was too much. Creating rumors of the father's suicide and scaring 15-year-old children was unacceptable.

Nanna got up from his chair and hugged his children. That day he decided to take a stand. He called the suspended cabin men and gatemen at his house. The investigation was still going on, but Nanna was yet to make an official statement with the commissioner.

He organized a small meeting at the house. They all studied everything they knew and found everything they could about the accident. Nanna even called the nearest station masters to know when the goods train arrived at their station. He investigated every minor aspect of the accident. The team spent a week preparing the statement.

"We have to be honest. We are not willing to get away with it. The driver had his responsibilities and we had ours. So we are going to write a formal statement to the commissioner," Nanna said to all the people sitting in the living room during the final meeting. They all agreed. Nanna and the team spend the whole day preparing a letter and noting the statements of each individual. He also mentioned that all of them are ready to face the penalty and are not trying to get away with it. He and the team handed that letter to the commissioner the next morning.

Because of his honesty, the commissioner and higher authorities canceled the additional penalties other than 6 months of suspension. Nanna had no problem with that. He agreed to the suspension period and signed the formal letter. He saved his and his team's job. As he was returning home, people from the neighbourhood were looking at him with awkward faces. Those were the people who started fake news about his suicide. He smiled at them with no hard feelings. That was my Nanna, he was extremely humble.

After the letter incident, railway employees from the neighbourhood started coming to him to get a letter written. Nanna would help them with any personal or professional problems. He would say, "Always be honest. Don't try to get away from your mistakes. But also don't suffer for something you did not do. Fight for your rights by maintaining dignity." That one incident changed his life. My Mom inherited his humbleness and she is the smartest and most practical person in our whole family.

I always admired Nanna's confidence. He was a man of honesty.

CHAPTER EIGHT

THE MISSED EXAM

Daund was a town where people working or studying in the city preferred to live. It was a peaceful town away from the city. Fresh air, no traffic, a cheaper lifestyle, and amazing people. There were plenty of trains connecting Daund to Pune. Trains starting from 3 AM to 9 AM were usually found crowded by working women, men, and college students. It was a whole different world. Regular train travelers treated each other like a family. Whoever comes first to the station would secure a seat for almost 20 other people. Running to the platform in the morning and catching a train was an adventurous life for students. My father was one of them.

Dad had a fun college life, with a massive group of friends who all were studying at Nowrosjee Wadia College, which was right next to the Pune railway station. It was easier to reach the college by a shortcut road from the railway tracks that opened at the back gate of the college.

Grandpa at the time had transferred back to Daund station as Chief of the Signalling Department. He got a 7BHK railway quarter especially designed for the chief officer to live. In a few years, Grandpa was going to retire from his job. Till then, that house brought happiness to his family. Daund became a favorite place, not just to Grandpa but to his children and later to his grandkids too.

Even though Dad and his siblings were studying in Pune city, they did not want to leave Daund. Instead of taking admission to the hostel; Dad and his siblings would take the train to Pune every day. Train timings were bizarre. The most convenient train was at 3 in the morning. Grandma's life had become all about getting up in the middle of the night to prepare lunch boxes for her children and husband. She never complained about that, although she would get dramatic at times. All the railway employees had a free family railway pass for a lifetime. Grandma wanted to travel through all the states of India. But Grandpa never had time for her. She would get mad at him for not taking her on even a small vacation. He would promise her every time she demanded a vacation, "I will take you everywhere you'd like after I get retired from the service." He did keep his promise later on.

Dad was good at Mathematics and Science. Grandpa wanted him to study in the science field. With good grades in junior college, Dad secured admission for a Bachelor of Science degree. The railway signaling department always fascinated him. To learn telecommunication, Dad chose electronics as his specialization subject in college.

While completing his degree, he was also studying for the Railway Recruitment Board exam. He would spend an hour or two at the college library to complete his daily study. His friends would wait for him and they all would take a return train at 6 in the evening.

On rainy days, the train schedule would go crazy. Majority of trains used to get canceled or delayed. In that case, Dad and his friends would spend a night in the college canteen having fun and studying for the next day's lectures.

Dad rather preferred staying in the canteen occasionally than at the college hostel. At the end of the day, he would look forward to going back home. For him, the home was the entire Daund town.

Back then, Dad never had to worry about reaching the train station on time. The quarter was literally 3 minutes away from the railway station area. Dad and his siblings would leave home when the train to Pune would arrive at the platform. Living in the railway quarter was a privilege. People could hear an announcement from their houses and leave for the station when they saw a train arriving in the railway yard.

One day, Dad had his exam at 8 in the morning. He decided to take the regular 3 AM train. Till the clock hit 2, he studied and got up to get ready. Usually, the train would enter Daund at 2:50 in the morning. That day, Dad did not hear any announcement about the train. He thought maybe it was running a little late. Half an hour passed but the train didn't arrive. Dad was about to call his friends when the landline phone rang.

"Hello?" Dad picked up the phone.

"Anand, it's me...Vishal. We have a major problem."

"What?"

"Next 3 trains have been canceled. Some issues at Yevat station. We have no train to reach for an exam before time."

"Now what?" Dad panicked.

"I am trying to arrange a vehicle.. a bike or a car. Will call you back."

"Alright," Dad replied, and hung up the call. Panicked, he woke up Grandpa and told him about the train. Grandpa had contacts with all the stations. He called a few of his friends to ask if any goods trains were going to Pune. Nothing. Dad had no way to reach college before exams.

Time was running faster. It was already 6 in the morning when Dad received a call back from his friend.

"I could not arrange any vehicle, Anand," his friend sounded disappointed and sad. "Looks like we lost this exam."

It was a final year final exam. Not only Dad, but all his friends who had no train to get to Pune had failed that exam.

Grandpa was very pissed at my father for being so careless. "I told you to at least get a hostel room during your exams."

"Sorry father," Dad apologized to Grandpa, disappointed with the whole situation. He could not undo what had happened. But he still had a chance to fix it. He applied for the re-exam, which was going to happen in two months. Meanwhile, he started searching for a job. He gave interviews at some private small companies and at the State Reserve Police Force as well.

Soon enough, Dad got a job as a clerk at the State Reserve Police Force for rupees 5 thousand a month. He would work a 9 to 5 shift and study for his final exam till late in the night. He was determined to make things right. When his final exam was a week away, Dad decided to arrange a place at the hostel. He applied for a week off from work and his boss agreed to give him an unpaid study leave. He packed a pair of clean clothes with his books and went to Pune.

My father was not so fond of the hostel room. But comfort was not his concern at the time. The day before the exam, his friends spent a night in Dad's hostel room. They all studied the whole night and went to the exam in the morning.

The exam went really well. Dad was happy and knew the final result would be great. He returned home after a week, which felt like a month to him. Without taking another day off, he reported to his work the next day.

The result of the exam came after a week. Dad had not just cleared the exam but got a good score. My Grandparents were really proud of him. Grandpa even brought sweets as his son had graduated.

Soon after the results, Dad got a pay raise at his job. He worked at the State Reserve Police Department for another 2 years while continuing to study for railway exams. The missed exam led him to his first job, which he still thinks is the best start to his work life.

CHAPTER NINE

CHASING THE DREAM

When you are determined to get a dream job and have a life that you have always thought about while growing up, the universe gives you the power to chase that dream. Dad was doing everything he could to secure the best rank in Railway Recruitment Exam. His job as a clerk at the State Reserve Police Force was good. The salary was decent, with regular work hours, and amazing colleagues. But it wasn't what he wanted to do.

"Why are you still here, Anand?" Dad's colleague asked him one day during lunch, "You always say railways fascinate you. Your eyes lit up when you talk about it."

"I need to clear the Railway exam first. The last exam wasn't good. I skipped the rank by just a few points," Dad replied.

"Why don't you leave this job and focus only on your studies?"

"I can't. I have responsibilities. Besides, I like it here. All the people working here motivates me."

"But your father is in railways, he can make a few calls and get you a job, can't he?"

"That's not how it is," Dad replied looking at his friend, "I want to earn that job."

My father decided to continue his existing job until he clears the railway exams. He started bringing his books with him. Whenever he got a free hour at work, he would start studying wherever possible. People would call him for a tea break. But he would politely decline and preferred to focus on his exam.

The railway exam was due in a week when my Dad applied for leave from work. He never used his holidays and sick leaves just to use them before the exam. On the day of the exam, he closed his books in confidence and said to Grandpa, "Be ready to read my offer letter." Grandpa patted his back and wished him luck.

When Dad was solving the exam paper, every question was putting a smile on his face. He could see his dream coming true. He was preparing for the exam for so long that the questions in front of him started feeling like old companions.

Just as he promised, Dad cleared the exam with a good rank. He was one step closer to earning the job he always wanted. Now he just needed to hear from the central railways about the offer letter. Till then, he continued his job. His friends from work were happy to hear about Dad's exam result. This time, Dad took his friends for tea.

"Tea is on me," announced my father, and almost the entire department joined to celebrate with him. He was happy and eagerly waiting for the offer letter. But little did he know, he was going to miss his current job and the people around him. He made good friends and learned a lot from them.

Soon enough, a letter arrived in the letterbox of Grandpa's railway quarter when Dad was at his work.

Grandpa opened the letter and as soon as he read it, tears rolled down his cheeks. He shared the good news with my Grandma who instantly decided to cook Dad's favorite sweet dish.

To surprise his son, Grandpa purchased *Motichoor Laddu* from the sweet shop and went to Dad's office. Dad's office building was surrounded by police officers. Grandpa had to show some ID and take permission from them to enter the office building.

A peon working at the office came to Dad's desk. "Anand sir, your father is waiting for you in the lobby, says it's urgent."

Grandpa never came to Dad's office ever before. This was unusual. Dad thought the peon is confusing someone else's father with his father. But he thought of checking it himself.

As Dad came out to the lobby, he saw Grandpa sitting on one of the metal chairs holding a box of Motichoor Laddu in his lap.

"Dad?" asked my father, confused but happy, "what are you doing here?"

"Son," Grandpa got up from the chair with a big bright smile on his face, "you got the offer letter, my son."

Dad froze for a moment. Grandpa handed him the offer letter which Dad scanned top to bottom with blurry teary eyes. He had been appointed as a "Signalling Technician" at Shahabad station in Karnataka state. Dad cross-checked his name once again, the position they were offering, and the joining date. It was his biggest wish written on a clean white paper in front of him.

Dad's journey at central railways was about to start. He finally had chased his dream.

CHAPTER TEN

TICKET TO THE DREAM

"All set?" asked aunt Aruna to my Dad when he was packing his bags. Dad received another letter from the Central Railways informing him about the training sessions he had to attend at Byculla in Mumbai. He would then have to join Shahabad in Karnataka for his first posting.

Dad was excited to go to Mumbai. Grandpa had been there for his regular interval training. He would always share his Mumbai experience with everyone. Mumbai marine life, the Gateway of India, popular markets, and Mumbai's famous Wada Pav. Grandma would always wonder about city life and ask Grandpa to take her to Mumbai. Dad knew she would demand the same from him.

"Yes," Dad replied, locking the last bag he packed, "all set."

"Packed snacks for the train?"

"Yes. It's in my backpack," replied my Dad looking at his little sister who was completing her diploma in electrical engineering back then. Uncle Anil and Uncle Anupam brought some fruits for Dad.

"Don't eat anything oily, Anand. Eat fruits," said uncle Anupam. He was working in a newspaper press. Uncle Anil was still in college pursuing his degree.

Dad packed the bag of fruits in his backpack and hugged both of his brothers and sister before leaving for the train.

Grandma was a bit worried for her son. What will he eat? Where will he stay? She kept asking. But she was extremely proud of him and she knew what the job at central railways would expect from him. She had seen her husband's hectic work and now her son was going to have to live that life.

Mumbai was around 5 hours away from Daund by train. Dad booked a ticket almost immediately after receiving the letter. As he boarded that train to Mumbai, he felt immense confidence. In a few hours, he was going to be in the *City of Dreams*.

Neatly tucking the luggage, Dad made himself comfortable on the seat. He looked around in the train compartment and saw a lot of people around his age. One of them approached him, "Going to Byculla?" the man asked.

"Yes. For the training," Dad replied, glad to meet a companion.

"Me too," the man grinned and took a seat next to my father. "What are you appointed for?"

"Signalling Technician. At Shahabad. And you?"

"S&T department? Awesome," said the man and introduced himself. "I am Arjun by the way. I will be taking the training for the Operational Department."

"That's great Arjun," Dad replied enthusiastically, "I'm Anand. Anand Pantoji."

Both of them shook hands and chatted for a long time. Talking about railways always made my father happy. A few more people joined them. They played games, chatted about the training center, shared lunch, and had a wonderful journey.

At around 8 in the evening, when Dad was having fun with his new friends, he heard an ear-soothing announcement. "Welcome to Chatrapati Shivaji Maharaja Terminus Mumbai, May I have your attention, please? Train number 11302 Up, Mumbai Bangalore Udyan express has arrived on platform number 3." A recorded voice made an announcement and repeated the same in Marathi and Hindi language.

Dad got off the train and was greeted by the fragrance of refreshing tea. Remembering his last tea with his friends from the previous work, he was missing Daund already. He looked over to his shoulder, his new friends were stretching their bodies after the long journey.

"Would you all like to join me for a cup of tea?" Dad asked.

"Of course. Sure," followed Arjun and a few more from the group. They all had an amazing cup of ginger tea on the platform with delicious Vada pav. They made plans to have a small tour in Mumbai while they were staying in the city. After having a quick snack break at the Mumbai railway station, they all took a bus to the training center.

The training center was a huge building. There was a large welcome board at the entrance displaying bold metal letters BYCULLA TRAINING CENTRE, CENTRAL RAILWAYS. The building had different workshop auditoriums and classrooms dedicated to signal technician training. There was a manufacturing building where parts of the signals were getting developed every day.

Dad saw that sign and a grin spread all over his body. He was excited to finally be there. When Grandpa told stories of Byculla, Dad always wondered about experiencing that life. And now, entering that building, he promised himself to be as good at work as Grandpa.

At the training center, all employees were divided into a group of two and assigned a room at the guest house. Dad had heard people talking about the guest rooms at the training center. "The rooms are amazing, and it has a TV installed on the wall," one of Grandpa's friends had described.

Dad got the key to his room and wondered who is going to be his roommate. As he entered through the door, a man was already sitting on one of the beds in a regular-sized square room. Two single beds were arranged next to the opposite walls with a window adjacent to them. A black and white TV was sitting on a table in the corner of the room. Two cupboards were kept next to the bed, with a tiny mirror attached to the door. The central wall had the door to the washroom and next to it was another door to the balcony. Dad loved the room, it was minimal yet perfect.

"Hello," said the man sitting on the bed, "Anand right?

"Yes, nice to meet you." Dad waited for the man to introduce himself.

"I'm Sameer, Sameer Vishwanathan."

"Anand Pantoji," Dad replied with a smile and shook his hand.

"So, where is your posting?" asked Sameer. "Mine is at Shahabad."

Dad happily informed, "Mine is in Shahabad too. We will be together for a long time then."

Shahabad is in Karnataka state. Dad could speak English, Marathi, and Hindi. But to survive in Karnataka, he had to learn Kannada.

Sameer was from Bangalore, and naturally, was fluent in Kannada. Dad and Sameer spent hours chatting, talking about trains and stuff, sharing their lives at home, and discussing the city they were in. Before leaving for Mumbai, Dad had purchased Kannada to Marathi dictionary thinking he would learn basic Kannada during his training sessions. He took out that dictionary and said to Sameer, "Nimmannu bhetiyagi santoshavaitu." Sameer laughed and replied, "Nice meeting you too, Anand. I will teach you Kannada."

A few years ago, Dad hated the thought of leaving Daund and living in the hostel. But as he was in his new world, he knew he was going to fill a bag full of memories. He kept the train reservation ticket in his wallet to cherish it forever. It was his ticket to the dream.

CHAPTER ELEVEN

ALL SET FOR THE WORK

"See you in a week then?" said Mr. Vishwanathan to my Dad who was busy packing his bags. The training was over with a final exam. The man had studied for the position in Railways for the last 4 years, clearing the exam was a piece of cake for my Dad. He enjoyed those 6 months in Byculla, met a lot of enthusiastic people and learned tons of new things. He also added some Kannada words to his Vocabulary from Sameer. The training days were exactly as Dad had expected, amazing.

His days in Mumbai ended with so many wonderful memories. Dad had gone to see famous tourist places and shopping markets in Mumbai. He had experienced marine life in the city. Dad and his friends would go to the *Chaupati* (Beach) almost every weekend.

He was supposed to report at his assigned location, Shahabad, in a week. Dad decided to go back home to spend some time with the family before going to Shahabad. As he came back home, he opened a large bag of gifts. Grandma was really excited. "My son got me a saree from the city," she bragged about it to her ladies' group. Aunt Aruna loved her new purse. He gifted cotton kurtas to his two brothers and Grandpa. They were all happy to see him home. He spent quality time with his friends from college, colleagues from his previous job, and with family for the rest of the week.

Dad did not unpack his bags, rather added some more clothes and snacks to the same bag. This time, he was going to a different state, 1200 kilometers away, which now is reachable in an hour by air. But back then, it felt far away from home.

The day arrived sooner than Dad had anticipated. He had a train to Shahabad on Saturday evening. After the 14-hour journey, the new place was waiting for him. He reached Shahabad early in the morning on Sunday. As he got off the train, Sameer was waving at him, "Hey Anand."

"Sameer? When did you arrive?" Dad was happy to see his friend.

"Last night. I was going to have some breakfast, thought maybe you'd like some?"

"Of course, sure." Dad followed his friend. Sameer took him to the nearest small restaurant.

"Eradu plates Masala Dosa please," Sameer placed an order. Soon, a delicious aroma of Sambar and Dosa filled the air.

"How was your journey?" Sameer asked his friend who was capturing the surroundings in his eyes. "It was good, no discomfort," Dad replied, taking a bite of Dosa.

After enjoying the delicious breakfast, both of them went to the guest house. Dad checked in and collected the key from the front desk. Sameer helped him with the luggage. "See you at lunch," he said and left the room.

The room was small, like a closet. One tiny bed was laying in the corner, not at all tidy. A small window was facing the railway tracks. For a normal person, that view from the window would have been a disappointment. But not to my Dad. He loved watching those tracks change into a crossing and trains arriving over those rails.

There was a tiny cupboard in the room. Dad could hardly fit his clothes. He decided to use his suitcase as his cupboard. There were one plastic chair and a table at the center of the room.

Dad decided to rearrange everything. He found a broom next to the bathroom door and cleaned every corner of the room. Then, he placed the table and chair next to the window, so he could enjoy tea and newspaper watching trains coming and going. Grandma had packed two clean bedsheets in his suitcase. He removed the existing bedsheet from the bed and spread the fresh sheet, the one still having a homely smell. As there was no pillow available, he used the other sheet for the pillow, folding it into a rectangle.

After setting up his small world in that room, he sat on the chair next to the window. Outside, a train passed by Shahabad, leaving the disappearing crowd of passengers behind. It was soothing.

Dad was set for his new job.

CHAPTER TWELVE

THE LEARNING PHASE

The excitement and a bit of nervousness were running through my father's veins. It was his first day at a new job with a team of Signalling Engineers. Dad woke up at 5 in the morning and took out one of the finest shirts and trousers for the first day, perfectly ironed. He had brought a small marble *murty* (statue) of Lord Ganesha with him. My Dad was the kind of man who would spend at least 15 minutes praying to god. Clearing up space on top of the cupboard, he placed Lord Ganesha's murty above a clean tablecloth and prayed for the blessing before heading to work.

"I will have some Idli please," Dad was ordering breakfast in the canteen.

"Enu?" asked the canteen man with his forehead wrinkling over his eyebrows.

"Idli?" Dad repeated.

"Haudu haudu," nodded the man and asked "Estu?"

Asking for idli was easy, but Dad could not understand the follow-up question. Thankfully, Sameer arrived for breakfast.

"Eradu plate idli sambar," Sameer said to the canteen man to which he smiled and nodded.

"Thanks, Sameer," said my Dad gratefully, taking a seat at one of the empty tables in the canteen.

"You will learn Kannada," Sameer assured, "You already know a few phrases."

"I'll try my best," Dad smiled and thanked the canteen man when he served two plates of idli.

When Dad told me about the incident, he described the Idli as one of the softest and best idlis he has ever eaten. He enjoyed the breakfast and wondered how his first day would go. He and Sameer reported to the station sharp at 8 in the morning. Dad, along with other new joiners, was waiting for further instructions. Soon enough, a man named Mr. Rao arrived and called everyone.

"We have to go to the relay room. Get ready," Mr. Rao informed and went to his office. He came back in 5 minutes with his assistant who was carrying a bunch of keys and led a team of 5 new Signalling Technicians for their first task. They all had to walk right by the side of the railway tracks, through the ballast (the crushed stones around the rail line). The relay room was a 10 minutes walk from the station. As they reached the room, Mr. Rao's assistant unlocked the front door.

There was a staircase leading upstairs, pointing to which Mr. Rao said, "You all will get a work desk up here." Then he led the team to the basement. The door had a board displaying the letters 'RELAY ROOM'. Dad had seen the relay room at Daund with Grandpa. For a normal human being, like myself, that room would be nothing more than a dull, closed, suffocating place ever. But for Dad, it was his passion.

Relay rooms have a double locking system. That means, both the S&T department and the Operational department (Station Master) put a lock on the room to ensure security. After unlocking both locks, Mr. Rao led the team inside. There were large cupboard-size boxes of wired circuits in the whole room. The mechanical lever frame was attached to a wall opposite the door. Those levers looked like rifles with color-codes describing loop-line (rail track adjacent to platform) and main-line crossing (central rail tracks). Everything in that room fascinated my father.

"Get to work then," said Mr. Rao to all the technicians. "You know the procedure."

"Yes, sir," replied my Dad and his fellows, and watched Mr. Rao leave the room.

"All the best," said Mr. Rao before leaving the basement.

Dad's job was to ensure the working of all the circuit tracks, mechanical levers, and basically everything that controls the signals. He cross-checked each circuit point and everything in the relay room was fine. So, unless Station Master reports any field failure, there was no obstacle in the way of the coming trains. That day, Dad went to fieldwork, made himself aware of all the relay points and signals. Whatever he had learned in the training session was practically taking place. He was having the best time.

Back then, there were mechanical signals with either a Lower or Upper quadrant system with three positions. The horizontal arm of the signal indicated 'danger' that the driver of the train must be ready to stop. Arm at 45 degrees in the upper or lower quadrant indicated 'caution' and the driver must proceed at the speed limit. And the vertical arm indicated the clear line.

Those mechanical signals would get difficult to notice during nighttime. So a man would climb the pole to light up kerosene lamps of green/red/yellow glass lanterns above the mechanical signal. This was a task of a great level of focus, communication, and alertness.

In the afternoon, the team went on a lunch break. Dad and Sameer went back to the same canteen at the guest house. The menu was fixed for the day. Bisibele rice, one of the famous dishes of Karnataka, along with sambar and leftover idlis from the morning. Post lunch, the canteen served rassam and Dad loved it. He told me, he used to look forward to having that rassam at the end of the day. He enjoyed the food, but he was craving Maharashtrian food. He wanted to eat roti sabji, dal-rice, pickle, and everything Grandma would cook. Especially sheera, his favorite sweet dish.

Apart from missing home-cooked food and language, he was enjoying Shahabad. People at work preferred Hindi over their native language. But when he would go out to the market, communicating with people in Kannada was not easy for him. He would take his dictionary in his backpack and explain what he needed in a few words to the shopkeeper. If Sameer came along, he would handle the talking.

On day 1, Dad spent the majority of his work hours understanding what he will have to do every day and in the case of failures. He had to go to the railway tracks too, for the signal inspections with the team. By the end of the day, Dad's whitish trousers had black patches of dirt from the fieldwork. He thought those stains were prizes of his first day's work. But he decided to wear dark-colored pants from that day onwards. He still does not buy white or light color pants.

From that day to the next 4 years, Dad learned a lot in Shahabad. He not just became smooth in signal management but also learned Kannada. Some days, he had to travel from station to station for day inspection or night inspections. Night inspections were not easy. The track area was not secure. Thieves would hide behind the fence to steal diesel from goods trains. They would throw stones at passenger trains just for messing around.

Sometimes, Dad and his team had to sleep in the waiting room at the station where there was no bed. They would arrange chairs and sleep till dawn. He became used to not having a pillow or blanket, or any sort of comfort in general. He had to go on double duties quite often, for which he had to stay on the field for more than 48 hours. It was hectic walking from the tracks on hot summer days which would get more difficult on rainy days. Winter fog was particularly challenging to work in fields.

He survived every situation without creating any technical errors. Mr. Rao was happy with my father's work. He even praised Dad's reports, his register was clean with a perfectly balanced sheet. "Your reports are perfect, Pantoji. Keep it up," said Mr. Rao.

"Thank you, sir," Dad replied, remembering how his uncle Aravind had taught him about numbers.

After spending four years in Karnataka, Dad returned to Maharashtra with a bag full of memories and a new language. When he talks about Shahabad, he remembers that small room, tiny bed, and food problems.

"Even though some things were uncomfortable, I loved those first 4 years of my job when I was learning new things. And I think, one must constantly be in the learning phase," he always says to me.

CHAPTER THIRTEEN

NEW OPPORTUNITIES

"It's good to be back," Dad said to Grandpa. They both were enjoying a cup of tea on a fresh evening on the veranda of Grandpa's railway quarter.

Between those years in Shahabad, Dad rarely visited Daund. He finally had some time to spend with his father. Grandpa's railway quarter was beautiful. It had 7 rooms and a large kitchen, almost as large as Grandpa's first railway quarter. The living room was decorated with some photo frames of Grandpa's achievements. A large sofa set was kept in the center of the living room. There was a beautiful garden in front of the quarter where Grandma would spend her early morning. She had requested a small Tulashi-Vurndavan (Holy basil plant vase) and a small temple for her prayers. She was happy with that house. By then, her kitchen had advanced equipment like a gas stove. She was the queen of her house.

"It's good to have you back," Grandpa replied, patting his son's arm. "How long till you have to leave for Kedgaon?" he asked.

"I am leaving in two weeks," Dad replied. Kedgaon was the small village where Dad had been transferred after Shahabad. It was just 17 miles from Daund, 15 minutes by train or 30 minutes by road. Dad thought about staying in Daund and taking a train to work every day. But his job was not 9 to 5 where he could follow the same routine. It was better to stay in that town. Kedgaon did not have a guest house like Shahabad. Department offered a small railway quarter to my father.

A week before joining Kedgaon Railway Station as a Senior Signal Technician, Dad enjoyed homemade food and Grandma's special dishes. As planned, he reached Kedgaon on Sunday afternoon by train. Behind the railway station, there was a lane of railway quarters. Each block had 4 quarters. It was like a rectangular house divided into 4 parts by walls and fences. Dad walked to his new home with the luggage he had brought. As he reached the block, he realized that he was the only one there. The rest 3 quarters were empty.

Taking the keys out of his pocket, he turned the lock and it clicked open. As he pushed the door, an unpleasant smell of the old house and a cloud of dust made him sneeze at the doorstep. Even though it was 2 in the afternoon, the quarter was dark. It was surrounded by lots of tall trees, which could easily make one wonder about horror stories. He went inside and found the switch. The room lit up and revealed its interior. It was just the 1-room-kitchen quarter, in terms of Railways, an RB-II quarter. Small living room/ bedroom and an even smaller kitchen. There were only two windows, one at the front adjacent to the main door and one in the kitchen. The quarter had a backdoor from the kitchen, opening to the backside of the block that was no less than a forest.

From the front door, one could easily see trains coming and going. There was a large water-well in front of the block, just a few steps away from the fence. People from the neighbourhood were filling their buckets with water. Dad went inside and checked the taps in the bathroom. No water came out. He checked the tap at the kitchen counter, not a single drop of water fell down. Then he realized why there was a crowd at the water-well.

Patiently, Dad cleaned the house and unpacked his bags. He then found an old rusted iron bucket in the washroom, which he cleaned first and took to the water-well.

"How often the bathroom taps don't work?" Dad asked a man filling his bucket from the well.

"You will get municipal water to your house taps twice a week. The water well saves you for the rest of the week," the man replied casually, lifting two buckets in his hands and tucking one pot under his arms. He seemed to be doing this for ages.

Dad saw the pulley attached to the well. A large strong rope was rolled against it. An iron water pot was tied to the other end of the rope. He pulled the rope to draw some water and poured it into the bucket and his water bottle. The water from the well wasn't clean. Thankfully, the stove in the kitchen was working. He boiled the water before drinking it.

In the evening, Dad took a walk in the neighbourhood. He walked past the quarters, to the main town. The central town was better than the railway quarter lane. There was a doctor's clinic, a grocery store, a vegetable market, and a temple nearby. He purchased some basic groceries like rice, lentils, wheat flour, and bought some vegetables. He also purchased a big can to store more drinking water and a clean bucket.

When Dad was returning home, he heard someone calling his name. A familiar voice.

"Anand," the man said. "Here, to your right."

Dad looked in the direction of the voice and saw a man in his mid-50s. He immediately remembered who he was. "Uncle Gokhale?" Dad grinned and waved at him. Mr. Gokhale was Grandpa's old friend from Bhusawal and was also working in Kedgaon.

"How come you are here, son?" he asked.

"I am joining as Senior Signal Technician, here in Kedgaon," Dad replied and touched Mr. Gokhale's feet to pay respect.

"That's excellent," said Mr. Gokhale and patted my Dad's shoulder in appreciation. "So, where are you staying?" he asked.

"Two blocks down. I got a railway quarter," Dad pointed to the lane.

"Ah. I used to live there too. My wife doesn't like those quarters," Mr. Gokhale shrugged. "So I rented a small place in the central town. It's not that far from here. Would you like to join us for dinner tonight?" he offered generously.

"Some other time, uncle," Dad politely replied. "I still have to set up a few things. Thank you though."

"Then how about this weekend...say 8 in the evening on Sunday?" Mr. Gokhale extended the offer.

"Sure. Sounds good. I will be there," Dad promised. He knew the man since his school days. Mr. Gokhale was like a family to Grandpa.

"Excellent. I will see you tomorrow at the station then?"

"Definitely," replied my Dad, and watched the man walk away to his home.

Dad was happy that he knew someone in the town. He did not expect his evening to be good. He came back to the railway quarter, to which he was struggling to call his home. Grandma as soon as heard about Dad getting a railway quarter, packed a separate bag with kitchen equipment. Dad opened the bag and took out two steel containers with a lid. He poured the rice he had gotten from the store into one of the containers and daal into the other. He had never cooked anything more than easy breakfast dishes or tea. But now he had to learn cooking.

Dad took out a large bowl and poured some wheat flour into it. He had seen Grandma making dough and rolling rotis. He started with the dough by pouring a random amount of water into the flour. As he mixed the two things, it became a soup. He added more flour. Then it became hard as a rock. After 5 overwhelming try-and-error attempts, something similar to dough was ready in the bowl in front of him. He then started rolling rotis. Meanwhile, a pan was set on the stove. He rolled an amoeba-shaped roti and placed it on the hot pan. While he was rolling another roti, he forgot to turn the first one. It burnt badly. Grandma did not like throwing the food away. Dad took out the burnt roti from the pan and served it on the plate. He was careful with the second roti which wasn't so much of a disaster.

Dad had purchased tomatoes from the market. He roasted one chopped tomato in the same pan and added some salt and his dinner was ready. Dad sat alone in that house and ate what he made for himself, a burnt roti and roasted tomatoes. He finished his dinner in silence, missing home and good food.

After dinner, he washed the dishes, arranged the ironed clothes for the next day, and went to bed. The day was tiring.

The next morning, Dad woke up at the usual time, got ready, and did his morning prayers and rituals. He made himself a cup of tea and had it with some cookies. He was ready to report to the new office. Locking the door of the quarter, he headed to the station. The station was peaceful. There was a very minimal crowd at the platform. First thing, he signed the attendance register and went to his cabin. Then he took a tour of the relay room.

Everything was pretty much the same as the previous one. Except, he was now a senior technician. Dad was excited about the new opportunity.

HONESTY AND ALERTNESS

The fresh evening breeze, the fragrance of flowers on the way, and the distant noise of playing children refreshed my Dad's mind. Walking by the market, he met a few of his colleagues buying vegetables. Greeting them and chatting for a couple of minutes, he walked past a temple to the nearby block.

As promised, Dad reached Mr. Gokhale's house on Sunday evening with some fruits. Mr. Gokhale greeted him at the doorstep with a bright smile, as if his own son was visiting him. Dad removed his shoes by the doorstep and went inside the house. The house was small but it had that homely touch. Photo frames, a small television, 4 chairs pointing to the TV, and a flower vase on the TV top. It was beautiful.

Mrs. Gokhale was cooking a delicious dinner. The fragrance of the food filled the house, traveling from the kitchen to the living room. She came outside, holding a tray of two glasses of lemon serbat. Dad touched her feet to pay respect and gave her a bag of fruits he had brought. She smiled with affection.

"I am glad you agreed to the dinner, son," she said. "How's everyone at home? Your parents?"

"They are doing well," Dad replied, "Mother is inviting you two to our home in Daund."

"We will definitely visit," smiled Mrs. Gokhale. "How's little Aruna? She is such a sweetheart."

"She is pursuing an engineering Diploma at Solapur. She stays there, at our uncle's."

"That's amazing, bring your family here sometime," said Mrs. Gokhale and went back to her kitchen.

Dad and Mr. Gokhale sat in the living room, chatting about work. Dad liked how he was referring to him as a son. He had seen the man working day and night in Bhusawal with Grandpa. The same man now had wrinkles around the corner of his eyes.

"How's life at the railway quarter?" asked uncle Gokhale, "are you adjusting to the place?"

"Pretty much sorted. Although, the place has water issues."

"Yeah, it does. And what about food?"

"I am cooking for myself," Dad chuckled as he saw uncle Gokhale laughing.

"I think you should get married now. Only a woman has the power and affection to turn anything into a home," uncle Gokhale suggested, smiling at Dad who did not think about marriage yet. Dad had no idea what to reply to that, he just nodded awkwardly.

"Son," said Mr. Gokhale, "Now that we have time, let me tell you," His tone was serious, "Some things you only understand as you get ahead in your job."

Dad was listening carefully to what the experienced man sitting in front of him was saying. He leaned back in the chair to make himself comfortable.

"There isn't a job without tension and stress. You know how night duty can be crazy right? People have different ways to deal with it. You must be careful with two things," he raised his index finger, "one, wisely understand people around you." He raised another finger, "two, be aware of politics at work. There is no work field without politics. You must stay aware all the time. " Uncle Gokhale finished talking and waited for Dad to digest the information. Grandpa had told him a similar thing.

"I will be careful. Thank you uncle," Dad assured him. They both chatted about their days in Bhusawal for a while till Mrs. Gokhale served dinner. She spread out a beautiful handmade rug on the floor and placed two plates in front of it. She decorated the plates by making flower *Rangoli* around them and lit up a small silver *Samayi* lamp next to it. Perfect Indian dinner.

Dad and Mr. Gokhale took a seat on the rug with a plate in front of them on which Mrs. Gokhale was serving food. She had cooked Rotis, Potato sabji, Dal-rice, Sheera, Pickle, Fried Pakode, and Buttermilk. Dad and Mr. Gokhale joined their palms to appreciate the food in front of them before digging in.

Dad took a bite of roti along with sabji and it was delicious. He smiled at Mrs. Gokhale, "The food is amazing," he appreciated. Both of them enjoyed the dinner while Mrs. Gokhale was serving them more and more each time they finished a dish. By the end of the evening, Dad's tummy was not just full of the food, but of the love he received. He discovered a home in those people.

Dad left Mr. Gokhale's house at 10 and walked back to his quarter. He was still thinking about how different that house was. Small yet beautiful. Mr. Gokhale felt like a guardian and my father was glad that he had a family in that town after all. He reached the block and looked at the railway quarters. There was darkness. No sign of a human being, except him. He had put in a request to get a quarter in another block with neighbours. But all the quarters were already occupied. Sighing, he unlocked the door. As he entered his room, dullness and emptiness reminded him of Mr. Gokhale's house and his words about getting married. He wondered how a woman can change this room into a house, it seemed impossible to him.

In that small town, his work was the only good thing he had. The rest was just an inconvenience. By the end of 4 months in that town, he got used to his railway quarter, the loneliness in that room. Returning home from work was never peaceful. He started spending more time in his office. Applied for more night inspections, so he could spend most of his time at work.

One night, Dad was inspecting each signal and a gate in the 20 Km radius of Kedgaon station in the middle of the night. He had two technicians along with him. Dad was very particular and thorough about the inspection. It was a matter of trains and people's safety. He checked all the signals on the way to the gate, fixed small errors, and noted down the details in the report he was preparing.

He and his team reached the gate protecting the neighbourhood. The gateman's duty was to close the gate 10 minutes ahead of the train's arrival, so no one from the neighbourhood crosses the rail line to reach the other side of the road. Dad saw the gate was open. He looked at his wristwatch, it was 2 AM and he knew there was a train due in the next 10 minutes.

"Sir," said one of the junior technicians, pointing in the direction of the gateman, "Sir, he is sleeping."

"What?" Dad went closer to check on the gateman. He was sleeping like a little baby. As Dad leaned forward, he immediately smelled alcohol. "He is drunk," Dad informed the team and asked the junior technician to close the gate and immediately inform the Station Master. The team waited for the train to pass by to ensure security. Dad tried to wake the man up, but the man was not even opening his eyes.

"Sir, let me try," said Dad's colleague. He opened a water bottle and threw some of the water on the man's face. Gateman stumbled at the seat and woke up. Dad watched him fall from the chair and struggle to get back on his feet. He was not in a state to guide the gate. Dad decided to wait at the gate until the next gateman showed up. Meanwhile, the other technicians took the man to the railway station.

Usually, in such cases, a police inquiry leads to the permanent termination of the job and even instant arrest followed by a jail period. But Dad decided to talk to the supervisor before doing anything. The gateman might lose the job, thought my father, and decided to be patient about the whole thing.

The next morning, Dad had to submit a detailed report to the supervisor. He thought about the incident. He knew, if he adds the alcoholic gate man incident to the report, the man will get suspended or worse. So, he decided to not file the report against the man and only narrated the incident to the supervisor. Dad, his team, and the supervisor interrogated the man who was crying and apologizing.

"I am sorry, but we have to suspend you for a month. You will be provided with the proper counseling. And for the time being, your salary will be reduced," said the supervisor.

"Sir, I am sorry sir." The man started crying, "it won't happen again, sir."

"You do realize what could have happened if Anand and the team weren't at the right place at the right time?"

"Yes, sir but..."

"You may go now," said the supervisor. The man glared at Dad with anger and walked out of the door.

Dad was praised for his work. But he knew, he had created an enemy.

After a month, the gateman reported back to work. He was given duty at the station instead of a gate. His pay was reduced and he was asked to not leave the station throughout the work hours. He had to agree for the sake of his job.

One afternoon, Dad was alone in his cabin. He was preparing the report to be submitted in the evening. The same gateman knocked on his office door.

"Yes?" My father asked, focusing on the task in front of him.

"Sir, I am bringing juice for everyone, would you like some?" the gateman said with too much enthusiasm.

"Sure, I will have some," Dad replied and resumed his work. After 15 minutes, the man came with a glass of orange juice and placed it in front of Dad. He smiled at my father like a good man and went outside.

Dad lifted the glass closer to his mouth and was about to take a sip when he smelled alcohol in it. He smelled it again to cross-check. It certainly was alcohol. He called the man in the cabin again.

"Yes sir," said the man.

"Please have a seat," Dad showed him the chair across his desk. The gateman panicked but took a seat.

"My juice happened to have alcohol in it," Dad said, keeping a calm tone. The man started to panic more, his forehead started sweating in fear.

"That is not possible sir, I gave the same juice to everyone," said the man, "nobody smelled alcohol."

"So, if I call someone to smell my juice, or send the sample to railway police, they would find nothing?" Dad firmly asked. The man started weeping. He threw himself on Dad's feet.

"I am sorry sir," he started begging. "Don't file a complaint, please."

Dad asked him to take a seat on the chair. The man obeyed and kept his head low.

"Why did you do it? Is this because I reported you to the supervisor? You know I had to, don't you? And you know how dangerous it is."

"Yes, sir I am sorry. I was angry."

Dad talked to him about how much awareness one needs to guard the gate. He listened quietly and nodded.

"I will not report you this time, just warning you," said my Dad to the man sitting guiltily across him. "You could just do your work honestly and carefully. Getting revenge wasn't the solution."

"Yes sir, I will never do this again and won't drink on duty," said the man honestly. He wrote an apology letter to my Dad later that day and thanked him for not reporting the incident. The man worked hard after that to gain back his original job. Dad requested the supervisor to revoke the penalty on him.

The gateman visited Dad in the railway quarter to thank him. Dad forgave him and told him to work honestly. The man left Dad's home with a smile on his face and promised to be good at work.

Dad then remembered why Mr. Gokhale was telling him to be careful. He learned a lesson, honesty in the workplace could backfire unless one is careful. Honesty had to be paired with alertness all the time.

CHAPTER FIFTEEN

'I AM FASCINATED BY THE TRAINS', SAID THE GIRL

"Do visit again," Grandpa bid goodbye to his friend with a bright smile. In two weeks, he was going to retire from his job at the Central Railways. The house was welcoming his good friends and colleagues every day. People were visiting him to give him best wishes for his life ahead. As he had to leave the railway quarter, he purchased a plot in central Daund where construction of our home was in progress. That quarter, which everyone adored, was soon going to be someone else's. Grandma didn't want to leave that house. But she was more excited about her own home that was being built.

One day, Mr. Gokhale was in Daund for some office work. He visited Grandpa at his office. Grandpa was happy to see his good old friend after so long.

"How have you been, Gokhale?" Grandpa asked, gesturing for his friend to take a seat.

"I am doing good. How are you? Heard you are retiring."

"Yeah... the farewell is on next Wednesday, you should definitely come."

"I would love to," said Mr. Gokhale. "Anand is doing good in Kedgaon. He is such a bright man, very smart."

"He is," replied Grandpa, his chest filled with pride. "He is living alone in Kedgaon for more than two years now. My wife and I are planning to find a good bride for him. It's time for him to get settled."

"About that," said Mr. Gokhale leaning closer. "I know a girl who would be perfect for Anand."

"Really? Who?" Grandpa curiously asked and told his assistant to bring two cups of tea.

While sipping tea, Mr. Gokhale asked my Grandpa if he knows Station Master Nanjkar. Grandpa was familiar with the name. He nodded, "I know him, but haven't met him yet."

"He has three children. The eldest daughter, Anjali, is a smart girl. She just completed her education in the Commerce field. Mr. Nanjkar is my good friend. I was recently in Madha for some work. He invited me for a cup of tea at his quarter and there I met his children. Anjali seemed practical, smart, and the perfect girl for Anand."

"And the other two kids? How old are they?"

"His second daughter, Asha, is still pursuing her degree. And his son, Avinash, is in 8th class."

"Alright," Grandpa said, thoughtfully, "What do you suggest then? How do we reach them?"

"I think you should send them a letter or I can get Nanjkar's office phone number."

"No no. Letter sounds good."

Grandpa talked about the whole thing with Grandma, who was happy and immediately agreed to send a letter. My Grandpa posted a letter to my Nanna on the same evening.

Grandma, already wondering about new sarees and jewellery for the bride, was eagerly waiting for the reply.

Meanwhile, in Madha, Nanna was searching for a groom who is not from the Central Railways. "Railway job is unpredictable. I don't want my daughter to marry someone from railways," he had made a firm decision. His own job had been a ride on a roller coaster. Naturally, he wanted a stable life for his daughter.

Back then, fathers used to arrange a wedding for their daughters as soon as the daughters would turn 18. But Mom was firm on her decision to complete the education first. She denied it every time Nanni talked about her marriage. Nanna and Nanni were a bit old-fashioned. They allowed their daughters to study, but not to get a job. Nanni would say, a woman should take care of her house and her children. Mom could not do much about it.

When Nanna received Grandpa's letter, his immediate response was, "NO. The boy is from railways, and that too the S&T department. He could lose his job, he could be an alcoholic. Who knows?"

Nanni just nodded. While Mom had no freedom to select her own groom, she was happy that her wedding is not going to happen anytime soon. Nanna decided to draft a letter to politely decline the wedding proposal.

The next morning, Nanna received a phone call in his office.

"Mr. Nanjkar, Gokhale speaking," came the voice from the other side. "I have been trying to reach you for two days."

"Why? What happened?"

"Did you receive a letter from Mr. Pantoji? About the wedding."

"How do you know about it, Gokhale?"

"I was the one who suggested the pair," replied Mr. Gokhale. "Anyways, what is your decision?"

"I don't want my daughter to marry the boy from the railways. So, I am going to decline the wedding proposal."

"What?" Mr. Gokhale was disappointed. "Maybe we should meet." Nanna hesitantly agreed to meet him in Kedgaon, at Mr. Gokhale's house.

The next week, Nanna took a train to Kedgaon. Mr. Gokhale was waiting for him at the station. Dad had no idea how many people were involved in his wedding plan, he was busy in his own little world. Mr. Gokhale and Nanna walked home.

Nanna was having a glance at the town on the way, he was observing where his daughter might end up if she marries Mr. Pantoji's son. He wasn't liking what he was seeing. Although, the town was similar to Madha. But a father's heart refused to admit that.

In the living room of Mr. Gokhale's house, Nanna was sitting in a comfortable armchair. Mr. Gokhale grabbed another chair and took a seat in front of Nanna. Mrs. Gokhale served some snacks and a cup of tea. As they were having fresh ginger tea, Mr. Gokhale began talking. "I have seen Anand since his childhood. He was a bright boy back then and still is. You know, people talk about him here, how honest and hardworking he is."

"Yes, but he is from S&T. You don't tell me you are not aware of that job. He would be constantly out of town. I don't want my daughter to end up alone, managing everything on her own. Besides, you know how hard our job is. Even I got suspended once. He could get too. I don't want a hard time for my daughter. My wife had suffered enough because of my job." Nanna hesitated for a moment and whispered, "And, he could be an alcoholic."

"I understand your concern," said Mr. Gokhale politely, "But Anand is not alcoholic, I am sure of that. And I don't think he will lose his job. Trust me."

"Nobody in central railways can guarantee not losing a job," Nanna quoted. "And I can't take a risk. If we go to his house now, I bet we will find alcohol bottles all over the place."

Mr. Gokhale thought for a moment, scratched his beard, and abruptly said, "Let's go check his house then."

"What?" Nanna jumped in shock. "No. I didn't mean it that way. That's not right."

"I am sure he won't mind," said Mr. Gokhale and literally took Nanna to Dad's railway quarter. As they entered the neighbourhood, Nanna was horrified to see the surroundings. 'My daughter can't live here,' he muttered. Dad used to keep a backup key to his quarter in his office drawer. Mr. Gokhale called Dad's colleague and asked to send the key and requested him to not mention anything to my father. When the key arrived, he unlocked Dad's house and switched on the lights.

Nanna was both shocked and impressed to see how clean and tidy the room was. Everything was in its place, not a single grain of dust in any corner. The living room was neatly adjusted. The kitchen was a bit messy but well organized. He and Mr. Gokhale checked every corner of Dad's room to find any trace of alcohol, but could not. "See?" said Mr. Gokhale, "he is not alcoholic." Nanna was still not convinced. He had doubts about the man he never met and that was totally understandable.

"Anand is perfect for Anjali, Mr. Nanjkar," Mr. Gokhale politely kept his hand on Nanna's shoulder. "I know you are worried for your daughter, but not just Anand, the whole Pantoji family are good people. Besides, Anjali seems smart and polite, she can adjust in a home; like sugar in water."

Nanna thought for a moment, had a glance around, and said, "I will talk to my wife and will reply to the letter."

"Take your time, Mr. Pantoji will understand. He too has a daughter who got married a year ago."

Nanna nodded and smiled. They locked Dad's room and went to the station. Nanna boarded a night train back home. He was still having second thoughts. But, this could be my daughter's fate, he wondered. The next morning, Nanna called everyone into the living room and narrated his visit to Kedgaon, including breaking into my father's house. He asked Nanni's opinion, who said her daughter is 23 now and must get married.

Back then, 'anyone older than you is wiser than you' was a phrase followed by every household. Even grownups had to agree to whatever elders were suggesting to them. Love marriage was a rare thing. Mostly, the father of the groom and bride would arrange the wedding before they turn 25 which was still better than 18. That was the age limit, after that, it was *"too late"*.

Nana announced that he is going to arrange the meeting with Mr. Pantoji and his family, to which Mom and Nanni nodded. Meanwhile, Grandpa announced Dad's wedding plan to everyone in the house.

~~

On a beautiful winter morning, two families were sitting together to decide the fate of a young man and a woman. Aunt Asha and uncle Avi had cleaned and decorated the living room of the railway quarter for the guests. Nanni was busy in the kitchen serving sweet dishes and snacks for the groom's family. Mom was wearing a beautiful red saree. Her hair was tied in a braid which she decorated with a few flowers from the garden. Dad was sitting next to Grandpa, wearing a clean white shirt over dark-colored trousers.

"Mr. Nanjkar, we already like your daughter. It's a yes from us," announced Grandpa with a smile. "It's your decision now, we won't mind if you ask anything to our son."

Nanna looked at my Mom, who was shyly sitting next to him. "I have no questions for your son, but I have a confession to make. I need to say this before you make your decision," Nanna said. My Nanna was a man of principles, so he shared the incident of breaking into Dad's room to check if he was an alcoholic.

After hearing this, Grandpa laughed and said, "I don't mind and I am sure Anand doesn't either. What you did was for your daughter, I would have done the same."

Nanna was happy with the soothing words of Grandpa. His doubt was long gone.

"I think we should let the bride and groom have a little chat in the backyard garden." Grandpa suggested, "They will get to know each other."

"I agree," Nanna replied, looking at his daughter. She was ready to have a conversation with my Dad.

Both of them went outside into the fresh garden that Mom had created and cherished for years. It was a little awkward at first, but they talked about a few things. Their hobbies and favorite movies. Mom was a big fan of Amitabh Bacchan, the movie star of the 70s, and so was my Dad. They talked about their college days. He asked what her favorite dish was and she replied anything vegetarian and less spicy. Dad chuckled at her genuine response, he liked her.

When they were talking about how Dad got his job in the railways, Mom said, "I have seen my father work hard for the railways. And it's amazing. *Railways fascinate me.*"

That's when Dad knew, this is the girl he wanted to marry. They talked for a few more minutes and went inside. Nanni called Mom inside the kitchen to ask her decision, Mom said yes to the wedding.

In the living room, Grandma whispered to Dad, "So? What's your decision? Do you like her?" He whispered back with a 'Yes'. A huge grin spread over the room and everyone's hearts filled with happiness. Nanni immediately served more sweet dishes. Grandpa and Nanna hugged each other, "We are going to be family."

Dad was happy and so was my Mom. Grandpa patted Dad's shoulder, "Congratulations, son."

Soon Mom and Dad's wedding plans bloomed in both houses.

CHAPTER SIXTEEN

THE WEDDING

"We want nothing from you, Mr. Nanjkar. You are already giving us your daughter," Grandpa said when Nanna asked him about wedding planning, gifts, and arrangements. "We will arrange everything for the engagement. You just bring our daughter-in-law."

"How about we divide the expenses?" Nanna suggested, a little stressed about the wedding.

"We can do that for the wedding. But engagement will be entirely organized by us." Grandpa firmly said, "Your daughter is a gem, don't worry about expenses."

Nanna was happy, he wasn't expecting this. He had been saving his whole life for the wedding of his children. He agreed to whatever plan Grandpa was proposing.

"The engagement will be in Daund, and my wife wants the wedding to be in Pune city if that's ok with you."

"Yes, we have no issues," Nanna brightly smiled.

"Our daughter Aruna is currently expecting her first child, so we have created a plan where she could be involved without any discomfort to her."

"We understand, Mr. Pantoji. We have no issues with either of the venues."

Mom listened to the conversation quietly. She did not like the fact that her wedding will not be in her own town, but there wasn't much opportunity for her to suggest anything. She saw her father withdrawing cash from the bank for her wedding plans, and she did not like it. She wanted to get a job to financially support Nanna as well as her future husband. But Nanna never allowed her or aunt Asha to have a job. He was old-fashioned that way. Mom wanted to share her thoughts on her wedding but could not. Instead, she preferred cheaper jewellery and sarees for her wedding to save some money.

On the day of the engagement ceremony, Grandpa was checking on all the arrangements at the venue. The venue was actually a public library for railway staff. Although, the event hall at the library building was not big enough to manage 200 guests. That's why a stage was set on the ground in front of the library. The open venue was decorated with flowers, lights, and a beautiful carpet.

Aunt Aruna and Grandma were taking care of the rings and things needed for pooja. The whole environment was filled with enthusiasm. Everything was set. Now they were all just waiting for the bride and her family to arrive.

It was almost 4 in the evening but the bride and her family didn't arrive at the venue. Grandpa kept checking his watch every 10 minutes glancing at the gate of the library. Every passing minute was raising panic in the whole family. Grandma was at the edge of an outburst.

"I think they called off the wedding. Anjali's father had issues with the boy from the railways. I think they are not going to come," Grandma cried, worried for her son.

"Don't say negative things," Grandpa snapped, irritated with the situation. "Just wait for another hour." But as another hour passed without Mom's arrival, Dad also started having the same thoughts as Grandma. They were about to shut everything down when Nanna rushed to the venue with his daughter and family.

"We are really sorry, Mr. Pantoji," Nanna hurriedly started to explain. "The train was ridiculously late. We could not contact you."

Grandpa and Grandma were happy that the bride's family had arrived after all.

"It's totally fine, we understand," Grandpa smiled and patted Nanna's shoulder. "There are rooms down the hall where you all can get ready."

Mom, Nanni, and aunt Asha went inside to get changed while Nanna was explaining what had happened with the train schedule to Grandpa.

Nanna had booked train tickets to Daund for the engagement day. The train was supposed to leave Madha at 5 in the morning and reach Daund in the afternoon. The engagement ceremony was in the evening, so Nanna knew they would reach on time.

Unfortunately, the train was late. They had no way to contact Grandpa as they did not have mobile phones. Nanna just hoped that Grandpa would ask about the train status and understand the bride's family was running late. When Grandma was panicking at the venue, Nanni was almost crying on the train. Nanna too thought the groom's family will call off the engagement. But Mom and Dad were destined to get engaged.

Mom quickly wore the yellow saree Dad had gifted her for the engagement. She loved the color. Putting on very little makeup, she tied her hair in a braid and wore the jewellery Nanna had got for her. Dad wore a black blazer and trousers over a white shirt and brown tie for the engagement.

Mom and Dad arrived at the venue where all the guests were seated. They exchanged rings and everyone cheered in happiness. It was one of the best moments in Mom and Dad's life. They were about to get married in the month of July 1989. Even though the train was the one responsible for discomfort and doubts in the engagement, the train was the biggest part of Mom and Dad's lives.

~~

Months flew by as the bride and groom's families went shopping, booked the hall, arranged caterers, and sent wedding invitations. The day of the wedding arrived a lot sooner. Grandpa had booked a small yet comfortable wedding hall in Pune city. It was slightly costlier than the one in Daund, but it had more rooms and better management. He wanted everyone to be comfortable at the wedding as it was a two-day event.

On 9th July 1989, the first event of the traditional Marathi wedding started at 7 in the evening. Mom was wearing a pinkish-red saree, gold jewellery, and green bangles which are mandatory for the bride. It's a sign of *Saubhagya*, which means a long-lasting healthy marriage. Dad was wearing a blue traditional Indian Kurta over white pants. There was a small Pooja called *Seemanti Poojan* followed by gift exchanging between two families. It was a simple event leading to a traditional dinner arranged for the guests. Mom and Dad were sitting next to each other and Grandma wondered how good they looked together.

Mom met Dad's side of the family and Dad met Mom's relatives. The *Seemanti Poojan* ended at 10 in the evening. The wedding ceremony was going to start the next morning at 6.

After Seemanti Poojan, Mom went to the bridal room, where she and aunt Asha was staying for the night. The rest of the family was in the adjacent rooms.

"Are you nervous?" asked aunt Asha to her sister. She could see Mom's feelings reflecting in her eyes.

"A little," Mom replied, removing her jewellery and keeping it safe in the box.

"So, you are leaving tomorrow, huh?" said aunt Asha, trying not to cry. "It will be just me and our little brother then."

"You can come and stay with me anytime you want," replied my Mom, cupping her little sister's face in her palm. "It's not like I am going too far."

"Will your husband allow you to come home and stay with us if you miss us?"

"I think so. I mean..." Mom thought for a moment, "I am sure he will let me visit you anytime I want."

"Okay," aunt Asha smiled, wiping tears from her face. Little did Mom know, married life is all about in-laws and she would get very little time to spend with her parents from now on. She laid down on the bed, tears rolling down from the corner of her eye as she thought about her home and the town where she grew up.

The next morning, Grandma came to Mom's room for the morning rituals involving the bride's pampering with a turmeric face pack, fragrant oils, rose petals, a new saree, and jewellery. Grandma gifted a brown-golden bridal saree to my Mom for the wedding day. Mom's eyes twinkled as she saw her bridal saree, it was stunning. Meanwhile, Dad was getting ready in the groom's room with his friends and brothers teasing and helping him to look good. He was wearing an orange kurta over a white dhoti (traditional Indian pants).

Aunt Asha helped Mom drape the heavy saree and put on the jewellery. Mom wasn't a big fan of makeup. She just applied a little face cream, some powder and dabbed a light pink lipgloss on her lips. Aunt Asha tied Mom's hair in a bun and rolled a beautiful tiara of flowers around the bun. Nanni was happy seeing her daughter in the bridal saree. My Mom was indeed a lovely bride.

Having a final glance at herself in the mirror, Mom arrived at the wedding venue where Dad was already waiting for her. He smiled as she sat next to him in the Pooja.

Dad put a beautiful gold *Mangalsutra* (bridal necklace) around Mom's neck and she became his wife. The wedding went on for another 2 hours, with all the traditional Indian rituals. Guests were praising Mom as she was smiling and talking to people who came to congratulate both of them. The wedding went smoothly followed by the *Shahi Lunch*.

On 10th July 1989, my Mom and Dad became each other's soulmates.

CHAPTER SEVENTEEN

THE FIRST HOME

Grandpa and Grandma were busy greeting guests at our new bungalow in the heart of Daund town. Grandpa left the railway quarter and started his retirement life with his wife in the new house he built for his family. The bungalow was decorated with flowers and carpets to welcome the new bride. The house was welcoming guests and neighbours every now and then for *Soonnmukh* (meeting and greeting the new bride).

Dad still had a week before resuming his work, so he decided to spend that time in the new house with his parents, siblings, and his new bride. Mom loved that house. It was a 2 BHK bungalow with a large terrace, a backyard where she could use her gardening skills, and a front yard where everyone could sit together for an evening tea. That house was perfect.

Grandma was sort of a strict mother-in-law. She asked the new bride to cook lunch so she could see if her daughter-in-law can make delicious dishes. Fortunately, Mom was an amazing cook since her school days. She could even make tough Indian sweet dishes that take years to learn. Mom cooked PuranPoli (a Maharashtrian sweet roti), dal-rice, two kinds of sabji, and some salad.

For lunch, she decorated the dining area with fresh flowers, arranged plates, and served the food. The fragrance of the food reached every corner of the house and Dad immediately knew his wife is a skillful cook and she can make his favorite Puran Poli.

Male members of the house arrived in the dining area. Mom gestured for them to take a seat and enjoy the food, while she was serving more Puran Poli. Anxiously, she was reading expressions on Dad's face when he took the first bite of Puran Poli. As soon as the sweetness of Puran rolled over Dad's tongue, making him smile, Mom knew he loved the food. Grandpa ate good three bites and said, "Everything is delicious. Puran Poli, perfectly sweet. Sabji, amazing. I think we should permanently give the Puran Poli department to Anjali."

Mom was glad to hear that. Grandma was happy that her son won't have to eat burnt food anymore. Although, in all those years, Dad had learned how to cook and had, in fact, nailed some dishes.

When Dad's holidays were about to end, he asked Mom to pack their bags as they had to leave for Kedgaon in two days. Mom had never been to Daund nor to Kedgaon. Nanna told her that Kedgaon is just like Madha, a small town. She was looking forward to setting up her own little house.

~~

"Is this Kedgaon?" Mom curiously asked when the train slowed down around Kedgaon station.

"Yes, we are here," Dad nodded.

"Already? I thought it will take at least an hour."

Dad chuckled and replied, "No, it's just 3 stations away from Daund."

Before going home, Dad showed her around the station, his office, and the cabin where he worked. He introduced her to some people, his friends from work. She spent a good one hour in Dad's office where he was arranging some papers for the next day. Dad asked for two cups of tea, and the office boy immediately ran to the canteen. He came back with refreshing ginger tea and some cookies. Both of them enjoyed their tea together talking about Dad's work and about the town before leaving for home.

"I am not sure what you are going to think about the house, but I have requested the new one," Dad said as they reached the railway quarter block.

"I have lived my whole life in a railway quarter, I am sure I can manage," Mom assured. But where she had lived was better than where Dad was living. She looked around the block, big water well, tall trees, half-broken fences, and no neighbours.

"Nobody lives in these houses?" she asked.

"No." Dad sensed a little fear in her voice but could not do anything. His request for a new quarter was pending forever. Mom entered the tiny railway quarter and abruptly screamed.

"What?" Dad, who was still at the door, immediately rushed inside, "what happened?"

There was an ugly lizard on the wall near the window. Mom was scared of wall lizards, she looked at her husband in horror. Dad waved the broom near the window and the lizard ran out of the house. Closing the window, he wondered, this was just a lizard, the house occasionally welcomed snakes and even red scorpions. He thought of telling her about these visitors but dropped the thought of scaring her.

Mom wandered into the house and decided to clean and rearrange everything. Cleaning the house and keeping things neat was her hobby since she was in school. She was very particular about what goes in which corner of the house.

That entire evening, my mother enjoyed setting up the small railway quarter. She had no complaints about the size of the house. In fact, she was happy that it was her home and she decorated it the way she always wanted.

Meanwhile, Dad had gone out to bring some vegetables and groceries for dinner. He always used to bring minimal stuff as he did not have a fridge. That evening he decided to get a small fridge, so they could store more vegetables and milk.

When Mom was satisfied with the house arrangements, she went to the kitchen and cooked a simple yet delicious dinner for the two of them. Dad wondered, the house had smelled the fragrance of actual food for the first time. He looked around the house. New fresh curtains, a flower vase on top of the cupboard, their wedding photo frames on the wall, and a neatly arranged kitchen. Remembering Mr. Gokhale's words, 'Only a woman can turn anything into a home,' he smiled at his wife.

Mom and Dad chatted about things to buy for the kitchen. Dad told her about the market and Mr. Gokhale's house.

After dinner, he took her on a walk to show her around the town. When they were headed back home, Mom smiled and said, "The town is no different than Madha." That town was their first home.

CHAPTER EIGHTEEN

KILLING THE FEAR

My mother settled into the new house within a couple of weeks. Every day, she would wake up with the Sun, tidy the house, prepare a lunch box for Dad, then do laundry and make tea for both of them. She made a routine for herself. Her morning would pass quickly. But for the rest of the day, she was on her own in that house. She wished for good neighbours, but the block was empty. Dad signed up for a daily newspaper for her and she would read it in the afternoon. But it wasn't enough to kill the time.

Dad's duty hours were uncertain. Usually, he would go to work at 8 in the morning and return late in the evening, or in the middle of the night. When he had night inspections, Mom had to live alone in the house surrounded by trees. It was no surprise that lizards or snakes would pay a visit once in a while.

Mom wasn't scared of the surroundings. She had gotten used to the tall trees and quiet dark nights. But she was scared of crawling animals. Every night, she would check each corner of the house if there are any lizards or a snake for that matter.

One night, Mom was alone in the house. Dad was gone for work in the morning and hadn't returned yet. There was no television or radio to give her company. She closed the front door, back door, and windows before going to bed.

The electricity was gone for hours. There was pin-drop silence in the house. She could only hear leaves of trees waving over the wind, the distant barking of dogs, and birds chirping.

Alone and anxious, Mom could not fall asleep. She was laying on the bed with her eyes wide open staring into the darkness. Suddenly, she felt something on her thigh. There was no way a blanket could move like that. She panicked, screamed, and jumped out of the bed. Thankfully, whatever it was, fell on the floor as she jumped. At first, she thought it could be a lizard and shivered in disgust.

Carefully grabbing the candles and lighting one with a matchstick, she started searching for the thing that crawled on her body. She bent down and held the candle under the bed. It was a snake, thin but of the length of one's arm. The hair on her neck and arms prickled with goosebumps as she spotted the snake.

Panic rushed through her body. Heart pounding louder, she was shivering and wanted to scream for help. Dad wasn't home, there were no neighbours to help her get rid of it. She sat on the floor, constantly staring at the snake. For a moment, she thought it was dead. But she could see a light movement on its body, probably breathing.

Hours passed. Dawn was still a few hours away. She was about to fall asleep on the floor when wax from the candle burnt her palm. She screamed and, before looking at the burn on her palm, looked under the bed for her company. The snake wasn't there. She stood up, scared, and sweaty. She again searched the house but could not find the snake. Maybe it was gone, maybe hiding somewhere else she couldn't reach, or on the bed. She checked the bed and shook the blanket. Nothing.

Finally, the Sun rose spreading colors over the horizon, and that morning Mom adored the sunlight. She opened the door and windows to light up the room. Electricity was still gone. She sat on the stairs and watched trains pass by. Soon the newspaper arrived, and for the first time, she read it right away. She thought of going to Dad's office to see if she can make any contact with him. But decided against it. 'It wouldn't look good,' she wondered and decided to wait for her husband.

Dad returned home at 9 in the morning. By then, Mom had cleaned the house, prepared the food, and finished God's Pooja after her bath. From last night, she constantly had a feeling of the snake crawling up against her body. She was scanning the room quite a lot. When Dad came home, he was tired from the night inspection.

"Did you sleep well?" he asked his wife with concern. She saw his tired eyes and replied, "Yes, I had a good night."

Dad did not suspect anything. He changed into his pajamas and was going to take a nap before heading back to the office. When he woke up from his nap at around 11, Mom asked if he would like some tea. He nodded yes.

Soon, the fragrance of tea filled the air in the house. Mom brought two cups and sat across from Dad on the floor. She was looking under the bed. Dad noticed and asked, "What's wrong, Anjali?"

"Nothing," she quickly replied. Mom hardly complained about anything. But Dad asked again. This time she told him about the snake, keeping a casual tone. She did not want to worry him. But Dad noticed the fear in her voice and felt bad for her.

"This house isn't that safe, Anjali. I should have told you earlier, I'm sorry. Snakes, lizards, and even scorpions are common in this area. I didn't know how to tell you without freaking you out."

She listened to Dad and asked, "How do you get rid of them?"

"I swing the broom towards the door, carefully from distance. It works for lizards. Snakes are a bit tricky," he told her.

Mom wondered for a moment if she could have used a broom to get rid of the snake. It wasn't a good trick, snakes could bite, she thought.

"I will get used to it, don't worry," she smiled. Dad got ready and again went to his office. "Take care, Anjali. And try to get some sleep," he said before leaving. Mom went to the market that afternoon to buy a portable lamp. The candles weren't comfortable.

From that day, Mom got rid of so many lizards. Of course, she was scared, but she had to do it by herself. She rarely saw a snake in the house, mostly when Dad was present so he handled it. That house, the neighbourhood was strange.

When she talks about the incident, she sounds confident, as if she killed a daemon. Even if not a daemon, she indeed killed fear inside her.

CHAPTER NINETEEN

MOM'S FIRST SALARY

"Dear little Sister…" Mom was writing a letter to aunt Asha after a long time. She liked sharing every little thing with her sister and hearing back from her. Mom wrote about her life in Kedgaon and how much she was missing her family. Putting the letter neatly into an envelope, she decided to go to the market to post it.

After posting the letter, she didn't feel like going home and spending the rest of the evening alone. So she decided to wander around in the market. In the central town, she found so many shops. Mom was not a shopaholic unless it was for saree. She loved buying new sarees. She saw a statue in front of the clothing shop draped in a beautiful silk saree. Unfortunately, she didn't have enough cash with her. Disappointed, she went to the temple before going back home.

The temple was soothing. She prayed to god and then found a place to sit. Some women were sitting under the tree near the temple, having their evening gossip session. One of them called my mother, "Excuse me," said the lady, "Aren't you Mrs. Pantoji?"

"Yes," Mom replied with a smile. "Anjali."

"Come join us. Don't sit alone," said the lady. Mom happily joined them. The ladies' group made some space for her to sit. She smiled and thanked them.

"So," said one of the women, "we heard you are a graduate."

Mom replied politely, "Yes. I am a commerce graduate".

"Lucky you got to study. None of us have studied beyond the 12th class. Either father or husband didn't allow us to get further education."

Mom did not know what to reply to that. She just felt glad that Nanna had let her study. She changed the topic by asking, "You all meet here daily?"

"Not daily, but often."

"Where do you all live?"

Some of them were living in the railway quarters, just a few blocks away. Some had their houses in the central town. Mom spent some time chatting with those women. They told her where to find the best quality groceries and which jewellery shop was good. Mom heard them talk about their lives, kids, and their houses.

"Tell us about yourself, Anjali," one of the women asked enthusiastically and Mom told them about her hometown, her siblings, and her new life in the town. How she spends her day alone by reading newspapers, tidying the house, and going to the vegetable market every alternate day. She blended into them as if she knew them for years.

After that, Mom often met those ladies at the temple or in the Market. One day, they were all talking about their children's exams. "My son...he does not study well. I have to yell at him 10 times a day. His teacher says if he doesn't score well in the exam, she would keep him in the same class for another year," shared one of the women, disappointed.

"Yesterday, I had to stop my gardening routine to take care of my son's homework. It's almost like I am studying on behalf of him," said another woman.

Mom listened to them quietly, nodding in between. As women were talking about their children's studies, one of them said to my mother, "You are a smart girl, why don't you start private coaching classes at your house?"

"Coaching? I haven't done that before," Mom replied with hesitation.

"Yes, but the kids are in school. You can teach them elementary Math and science. It would be really good. Besides, you spend the whole day alone, this will pass your time too," suggested the group of ladies.

Mom thought about it for a moment and replied, "I will ask my husband. If he agrees, I guess we can start."

Women grinned. Mom really liked the idea. She even started dreaming about teaching kids. That evening, while she and Dad were having dinner, Mom politely started the conversation, "I need to ask you something."

"Yeah, what is it?" Dad asked, still focused on the meal.

"So I have these friends...women from the neighbourhood," she started telling him about her evening, "They suggested that I should start coaching classes for kids in the neighbourhood. Their kids need help with studies."

"Where would you take classes?" Dad asked, looking at her.

"Here. In our house," she replied, slightly panicked.

"And when are you going to start it?" Dad sounded a bit serious.

"I haven't decided yet...I thought...," she replied hesitantly and was convinced that Dad would not agree.

"I think," Dad replied thoughtfully, "you should start it as soon as you can. Tell your friends tomorrow that they can send their kids. It will be good for you as well." Dad smiled at Mom. She could not control her excitement. She thanked him and started planning when and how she is going to do this.

The next evening, she met her friends at the temple. They all were already waiting for her.

"So?" asked one of the women, "did your husband agree?"

"Yes," grinned my Mom, excitedly, "he said I can do this. You can send your kids tomorrow morning, at, say 11?"

Women were happy to hear that, they all agreed to the time.

"What about the fees?" asked one of them. Mom hadn't given it any thought.

"Oh. Umm...I don't know," she said, "I will teach them free of cost."

"No no. We don't want you to take so much effort and not get fees. We will see how much we can pay?"

"No problem, it's alright," replied my Mom and thanked them for the great idea. Women blessed her and gave their best wishes.

~~

The next morning, Mom prepared Dad's lunch box and got ready earlier than usual. She was excited about her first batch of coaching classes. Dad wished her luck and left for his work. Mom cleaned the living room again and found a beautiful carpet that she spread over the floor for the kids to sit on. She had also brought some cookies for them.

The clock on the wall showed 15 minutes to 11 in the morning. Mom was expecting around 4 to 5 kids to appear. The First 2 kids arrived with their mother. "Anjali, both of my sons are joining the classes. This is Rahul, he is in 2nd grade and...” she pointed to her other son, “this is Utkarsh, 5th grade.”

Mom smiled at both of them and asked them to come in. Before starting the coaching, she asked them about their favorite subjects, school, friends, and what they play in the evening. Kids got along with her and talked to her as if she was their friend. Mom was just 24 and had the magic to make kids love her. After 10 minutes, 15 kids arrived out of the blue. She had not expected it. Some of them were in 8th grade and brought all their younger siblings along. She did not have enough space to occupy all of them. She spread two more carpets on the floor on which kids squeezed themselves and settled down. She sat on the bed so she could see all of them. One by one they introduced themselves. Mom asked them similar questions she had asked the first two kids and they answered enthusiastically.

For the first day, Mom divided the kids into groups based on their classes. She then started with mathematics. She asked the older kids to solve the math problems they already knew until she taught little kids and gave them some tasks. Older kids were quiet and cooperative.

She started teaching kids from 2nd to 4th grade, helped them understand different ways to solve the same math problem, and gave 10 problems for them to solve by themselves. While they were on it, she diverted her teaching to kids from 5th to 8th grade. One by one she taught a math concept to each group and asked them if they understood it. Some of them nodded yes and started to solve more problems. For those who said no, Mom formed another tentative group for them and again explained the same math problem in a simpler and slower way. After a few attempts, they got along.

Kids liked how my mother was easygoing around them. She wasn't scary strict but strict enough that kids would respect her. After two hours, the kids finished their homework, and Mom checked their notebooks. She was happy that her students did well on the first day.

To appreciate their efforts, she brought out cookies on a large plate. Little kids started dancing in happiness while the older ones smiled. They all enjoyed those cookies and a few minutes of relaxation. Before going back home, Mom gave each of them some homework, "I will check it tomorrow at the same time. See you then, bye kids," she waved at them and watched them run away in happiness.

She had a good time after so long. Those two hours in the morning were a bit tiring but happier. She folded all the rugs and carpets neatly and kept them in handy for the next day. For the first time in a while, she did not feel lonely while having her lunch as her thoughts were traveling back and forth among those kids.

After that day, the news of my mother's coaching classes travelled through the neighbourhood and the whole town. More parents visited Mom to enroll their kids. She accepted each one of them. She would ask parents to give her a moment alone with the kids so she could ask them some questions to better understand them. Kids would not speak from the heart in front of their parents. Maybe because they were scared or uncomfortable. Mom would take them out in the front yard and walk with them. Kids would speak to her about their favorites and dislikes. She would listen very carefully and plan her teaching method accordingly.

By the end of the month, the parents sent the coaching fees with their kids. Mom had not asked for money. But they generously sent Rs. 200 per child for a month of teaching. Mom received her first salary. She kept the money in front of god and prayed from her heart. When Dad came home, she told him about the salary. He was happy and proud of his wife. "Get yourself whatever you want," he said.

Mom went to the market the next evening. She again saw the silk saree that she had adored a month ago. Now she had her own money. She thought for a moment and entered the shop. Turned out, the saree wasn't that costly. In the same shop, she saw a blue casual shirt and thought it would look good on Dad.

When Dad and Mom were sitting in the living room after dinner, she handed him the gift and showed him her own saree too. Dad loved it. He tried the shirt on and it fit perfectly. He wore that shirt for his work the next day. Mom too wore her saree and looked in the mirror. She looked beautiful. She had earned it.

CHAPTER TWENTY

TALK TO YOUR KIDS

When you pour your heart into something, with whole dedication, the results are always wonderful. My mother was succeeding in her coaching classes really well. Her students and their parents positively talked about her with their friends. Every month, more parents enrolled their children and soon my Mom became as busy as my Dad.

She purchased a portable blackboard and turned the living room into tuition. As the student count grew, she made batches. Little kids from 1st to 4th grade had their school timing from morning 7 to 11. Mom set their batch for the afternoon from 2 to 4. Kids from 5th grade to 8th grade had afternoon school timings, so Mom created morning batches for them. The timings were convenient for all the students.

My Mom was very patient with the kids. She never yelled at any of them or scared them away. She would solve their problems no matter how many times they asked the same doubt. To make them understand the concept, she would give real-life examples. Mom initially started with just Math and Science but eventually grew her niche. She later began teaching history, languages, and geography as well.

Mom purchased syllabus books for all grades. Whenever she had free time, she would study and prepare notes. Soon enough, the parents of the students who had improved their scores started visiting to thank her. Mom became more famous in the town. People started talking about her, "Since my kids are taking classes from Anjali, they scored well than the last exam. She is a really good teacher." Dad was proud of his wife.

In 1990, Mom was 4 months pregnant and was soon expecting her first child. Dad thought the coaching classes might get overwhelming for her. But she said, "I love being with kids. Our baby will listen to what I am teaching. And maybe, just like Abhimanyu heard how to enter *Chakravhyuha* when he was in his mother's womb, my child will learn some math and science equations. You never know."

Dad laughed and said, "Okay. But you have to be careful. And take proper rest as well." She nodded and promised she would take care of herself.

One day, after her morning batch, parents from the four blocks down the street came to see my mother with their son. The boy seemed a little lost. Mom made some tea for the parents of the kid and asked the boy if he would like some milk. He said nothing. Mom brought the milk anyway, and some snacks. The kid didn't drink the milk nor did he pick up anything from the plate of snacks. Mom was worried about him and thought if he was unwell.

"He is in 3rd grade, Madam," the father of the boy began talking. "He is having a hard time with his studies. His grades have fallen and he does not understand a word they teach in school."

"He can't even read properly," added his mother. The boy was sitting quietly with his face down.

"But he is just a kid. Some kids need more time and eventually understand everything. How was his performance in 1st and 2nd grade?" Mom asked, looking at the little boy.

"Not good. But the teacher did not fail him," replied the father. Mom listened to the parents carefully as they explained his situation. She was confused and wondered what could be wrong with the kid. She thought he needs counseling or some therapy, but didn't say anything. Those two words are not well received by people from a small town.

"Do you mind if I take your boy for a little walk in our front yard?" Mom politely asked the parents.

"Not at all, we could go out if you want. You can talk to him in the house," said the boy's mother looking at Mom's pregnant belly.

"No no, you please feel comfortable to grab some more snacks and enjoy the tea."

She asked the boy to hold her hand. He hesitated but eventually got along. She took him out and asked if he would prefer a walk or wanted to sit at the stairs. As he didn't reply, she decided to walk with him.

"So, What is your name little one," she asked looking at the small boy holding her hand.

After a long pause, the kid replied, "Mayur."

"That's a good name." she smiled and asked, "You don't like milk?"

He nodded. "Is that a yes or no?" she asked.

"I like the milk, but not so warm," finally the kid was talking.

"Oh. I will get lukewarm milk for you."

He nodded again. Mom could see, he was normal but was scared about something.

"What is your favorite game?" she asked, looking into his twinkly little eyes.

"I like to play peek-a-boo and my toy cars," the little kid replied.

Mom kept asking about his likes and dislikes. "Do you have friends in school?" She looked at him, and suddenly he seemed scared. She could feel his grip on her palm getting tighter.

"Is there any problem little one?" she asked and he abruptly started crying. She held him close and let him calm down at his own pace. The kid replied through his sobs, "I have no friends. They are all bullies."

Mom's heart broke. She brushed her fingers through his hair.

"Do they tease you or hit you?" she asked and regretted wondering if the question wasn't right for the kid. But he replied, "They tease me, never sit with me during lunch break, and sometimes even hit me."

The kid opened up to my Mom and she listened like his mother. After a moment, she hugged him and said, "I will talk to those kids okay? Let's get you some milk." The boy nodded and walked back home with her.

When Mom returned with the kid, she saw his parents waiting for her impatiently. She apologized for taking so long and asked, "Would you like some more tea? " They nodded yes.

"Could you help me in the kitchen?" Mom politely asked the boy's mother and the lady was happy to help.

"When's your due date?" Mayur's mother asked, looking at Mom's glowing face. Pregnancy made her prettier.

"In the first week of July," Mom smiled and started making tea for the three of them and lukewarm milk for the little boy.

"I need to talk to you about your son," Mom gently started the conversation, and for a moment Mayur's mother panicked seeing her serious face.

"Yes?" the lady asked.

"He is being bullied in his school. Did you know that?"

The lady looked puzzled. "He never said anything to us."

"Or maybe you didn't listen?" Mom firmly said, looking straight into the woman's eyes. "Don't get me wrong. I know you have a better experience with children and I am yet to start that life. But you need to listen to him. Ask him questions. He is scared. He is so small and being scared is not good for him. Please talk to him. Go to his school. Talk to his teachers about the issue. I will help him in scoring good marks. But you need to help him solve the problem he is having in school or his life for that matter. Promise me you will?" Mom was talking nonstop in panic and went out of breath. She drank some water and calmed herself down. The lady had tears in her eyes. She did not even know what her boy was going through.

"It's not too late yet. When you go home, spend time with your kid. I know it's hard to manage everything. But kids are our priority. Tell him bedtime stories, and ask if anything is bothering him," she said, pouring tea in three cups and milk for the boy in a glass with a spoon full of chocolate powder. She and the boy's mother went back out to the living room. Mom sat next to Mayur and said, "I made you some chocolate milk. It's lukewarm. You'll like it." The boy smiled at her.

"He can join the afternoon batch from tomorrow. If that's not a problem?" Mom suggested, looking at the parents who were now sitting quietly.

"Actually," the father of the child hesitantly said, "We want you to pay extra attention to him. We are willing to give extra fees." Mom thought for a moment. She looked at the boy who was now enjoying his milk. She smiled and said, "It's not about money, sir. I will be happy to teach him. Send him here at 4 in the afternoon."

Afternoon 4 to 5 was her nap time. But she decided to give that to Mayur who needed her help more than anything. Parents agreed. "Thank you, Anjali," said the lady and hugged my mother. "Take care. Let me know if you have any food cravings," she smiled.

Mom blushed and said, "I will definitely tell you." She looked at the little boy who was now holding his father's hand. "See you tomorrow, Mayur," she said waving her hand and the kid waved back at her.

She stared at the road, at Mayur, until the three walking figures faded along the path. That day Mom decided, she would change that boy.

CHAPTER TWENTY-ONE

A Caring Neighbour Next Door

"Alright students, same time tomorrow," Mom handed over the notebooks of students as they were all busy packing their bags. "And finish your homework, okay?" The hour-hand on the wall clock hit 4, it was time for little Mayur to show up. She had a glance at the path in front of the block and saw Mayur's mother rushing to drop him at the class.

"Sorry Mrs. Pantoji, we are a little late," Mayur's mother apologized while gesturing for him to go ahead.

"It's alright," smiled my Mom, looking at the kid whose eyes were puffy red. "Looks like someone had a good nap," Mom laughed and Mayur's mother joined in.

"He doesn't sleep this late, but he had some activities in school."

"No worries," Mom gave Mayur a comforting smile. Mayur's mother went back home saying she will return in an hour or so to pick him up.

Mom asked Mayur to take a seat on the rug while she was cleaning the math equations on the blackboard from the previous class. He waited for his teacher to settle down. She smiled and said, "Let's start with the language class, shall we?"

The kid nodded and pulled out a textbook from his yellow backpack which had Tom and Jerry's photo print on it. The way he was handling the bag made my Mom smile as it was almost as big as him. He probably loved the bag because of the cartoon print.

She began with the basic spellings and asked him to repeat after her. "A P P L E- Apple," she pointed to each letter while he listened to her. Mayur repeated after her. He was in 3rd grade. There wasn't much to teach. Mom thought he was doing well until she asked him to write. He couldn't. She thought maybe it was because of English, so she asked him to write his own name in the Marathi language. He just stared at the blank paper. Then she understood, he hasn't learned to write well yet. He could write a few random letters, but that was seldom.

Mom asked him to read a few letters from the textbook. He could not. So it was clear that he needed help with almost everything. When Mom was asking him to repeat the words from the board, he could do it. But when it came to writing or reading something different, he was struggling. Mom patiently taught him to write his name in that one hour. The boy tried his best to turn his wrist and roll the pencil on the paper to write the letters.

Mom was constantly reminding him that it's okay if he can't do it, she will teach him again. An hour flew like a few minutes and Mayur's mother arrived to take him home.

"How did he do?" asked his mother.

"He did very well. In fact a little more than well," Mom replied, patting him on the shoulder. He seemed happy. It was probably the first time he had heard someone talk something good about him to his parents, or in general. His mother thanked my Mom and said, "I appreciate you taking an effort for my child," she held Mom's palm and squeezed it a little to show that she was glad.

Every day, Mayur would show up at 4 in the afternoon. Mom slowly moved ahead and taught him the alphabet. She wrote letters in his notebook and asked him to trace those letters. This activity went on for a week. Some days, he would say he was bored with the alphabet, so Mom would teach him numbers. Some days, she would just tell him a small story with a moral and he would enjoy those little breaks in the study.

She gradually took his classes to the next level. It was the month of April, children had their final exams in a week. Mom was conducting practice exams for all her batches. She had prepared question papers by herself and each day kids would sit either in the living room or in the front yard to solve the papers.

Mom designed a special test for Mayur. She wanted to see how he performs. His question paper was a little easier than others from the same grade. She watched him try his best to write the letters. And he not only wrote letters but also read short sentences. He actually did good and almost solved the whole question paper. However, there were some things he needed to improve. Mom still had a week to prepare him for the exam. The rest of the children did amazing, some of them even scored full marks in the practice exam.

My mother asked Mayur's mother if he could stay for half an hour extra for the rest of the week. She agreed without any questioning as she wanted her child to perform well in exams. Mom worked hard on his weak areas. She used new techniques to teach him. Words he couldn't read, she asked him to write those words 10 times. Every time she taught him something new, she would explain the meaning in Marathi and show him real examples, things he could see and then learn. He was getting better. He was doing pretty well in math as well. The good thing was, that little kid was as much determined to learn as my Mom was to teach him.

When the exam was a day away, Mom didn't take any study revisions. She took a special relaxation session where she talked to kids and played small games that indirectly involved brain teasers. Kids loved her for being such a lovely teacher. She wished them luck and offered cookies as a prize for their scores in the practice exam. Students bid her goodbye and went home. For the next 10 days, they had their final exams.

~~

When Mom was living her new life as a teacher, Dad was getting busier at work. The majority of his work was maintaining the electromechanical signals. Sometimes a small error in wiring would cause signal failures. In such cases, manual signaling was the backup solution. Drivers and the assistant drivers of the train were trained to pay attention to both the signal pole and the man who usually would stand alongside the tracks to wave the red/green signal flags till the driver waved back at him with the confirmation.

If any problem occurred, Dad would abruptly rush to board the first available train to go to the station in the proximity of his division to solve the error. He did not have a mobile phone to contact Mom to inform her that he was leaving the town and it could take a few hours or even a day to return. But she was used to it. If Dad didn't return, she would assume he was working out of town. Sometimes, someone from Dad's office would knock on the door to inform his whereabouts.

Dad's fieldwork wasn't easy. It involved a lot of risks and overexertion. The train was his second home. His work asked him to spend more time on trains or on tracks than at his house. He was worried about Mom as she was seven months pregnant by then. Once in a while, Mrs. Gokhale used to pay a visit with delicious food for Mom. But her home wasn't next door. More often, Mom would spend nights alone and Dad wished for good neighbours to at least give her company when needed.

One fine morning, when Mom was taking a walk in the front yard, a family of four was unlocking the adjacent railway quarter. A couple in their mid-forties and two sons between ages 10 to 12. Mom curiously looked at them and asked "Are you moving in here?" The wife came closer to the fence and replied, "Yes. My husband got transferred here."

Mom grinned with excitement, "I am Anjali. Welcome to the neighbourhood," she smiled at the woman and her kids.

"I am Lakshmi Patil, these are my sons Amol and Akash." The new neighbour introduced her kids. Mom waved at them.

"So when is the due date?" asked Mrs. Patil as Mom's belly was noticeable.

"Around 10 weeks," Mom replied blushing a little. While two women were chatting, Mr. Patil and his sons had taken all the stuff inside. They were already arranging the house.

"Would you all like to come for tea?" Mom asked the new neighbour. "You must be tired. Besides, you need to set up a house."

"Oh, no no dear," Mrs. Patil lightly patted Mom's shoulder. "We don't want to bother you. In fact, you should come for tea."

"Do you need a hand in setting up the kitchen? I am free, I could help," my mother suggested. But Mrs. Patil was concerned about her.

"You can just give me company if you like," Mrs. Patil smiled. "But I don't want you to help me. You should take proper rest." She gestured to my Mom towards her house, "come on in, I will make refreshing tea for you."

"But you have to set up a kitchen yet," Mom asked.

"Oh don't worry about that. We have got everything. My husband has been transferred 3 times in the past 4 years. I am used to setting up new houses. My sons are probably arranging the stuff already." Mrs. Patil insisted my mother come for a cup of tea. She noticed that my Mom was alone in the home and felt worried for her.

Mom went in and was surprised to see that the kids had already cleaned the house and were now unpacking the kitchen utensils. Mrs. Patil pulled out a folding chair from her luggage and asked my Mom to sit in the kitchen while she made some tea for everyone.

Mom sat down and observed Mrs. Patil effortlessly moving into the kitchen. Mrs. Patil was no less than a machine. While tea was boiling, she arranged the grocery boxes behind the stove. Then she quickly cleaned the racks before setting up all the utensils. The woman seemed to be an expert in the kitchen.

Mrs. Patil poured tea into 5 cups. Puzzled to see the number of cups, Mom asked, "Kids drink tea too?"

"Yes. They hate milk. So I allow them some tea once in a while."

Amol came to the kitchen and took three cups out in the living room for his brother, father, and himself. Both the kids seemed strong and a little extra mature for their age. Mom and Mrs. Patil were enjoying the tea in the kitchen. She asked my mother about the town, the neighbourhood. Mom wasn't new to the town anymore. She told Mrs. Patil about the best school where she could send her sons, the market, temple, grocery store, and almost everything like a native citizen of Kedgaon. Mom wondered how she got along with the town, mostly because of the women in the neighbourhood and of course, her students.

"So, what do you do all day?" Mrs. Patil asked wondering how a 7-month pregnant woman stays alone all day in this insanely quiet place.

"I teach children from the neighbourhood," Mom replied, taking a sip of the tea. "Now they are enjoying the summer holidays after the final exams. Classes are paused till school reopens."

"You are a teacher?" Mrs. Patil asked curiously.

"Yes," replied my Mom with a smile, "I take coaching classes for kids."

"Where? In your house?"

Mom nodded.

"That's amazing. I sensed you are a smart girl at first glance," grinned Mrs. Patil. "Do you take classes for 6th to 9th-grade students?"

"Yes. I even have 10th-grade students. I prepare them for board exams."

Mrs. Patil seemed to give it a thought and said, "Can my children join your classes?"

"Of course. Why not. I have batches for 5th to 10th grade in morning hours."

"That sounds perfect. I will ask my husband," said Mrs. Patil and smiled in relief. "Both of my sons are already good at studies. But they are lazy to finish day-to-day homework. Besides, I never went to a school, so I cannot help them much. It's great that you can teach them."

"Of course, I would love to. And both of them will quickly find new friends too," Mom gave an assuring nod and helped Mrs. Patil chop some vegetables.

Mrs. Patil looked at the young woman sitting in front of her and saw how confident she was. Mom spent around an hour with the new neighbour before going back home.

For the first time in years, Mom did not feel alone in that house. She had a caring neighbour next door.

CHAPTER TWENTY-TWO

TREMENDOUS KNOWLEDGE AND EXPERIENCE

Sundays are relaxing holidays for nearly everyone. It's the only day people look forward to during the week. A day to enjoy and brace ourselves for the coming week. Unless you are from the S&T department of railways. Then there are no holidays, every day is a workday. My Dad used to go to work on Sundays at odd times and he had to travel a lot in his section. He had to be alert and ready to go for an emergency whenever needed. A man from his office would show up anytime to call him on emergency tasks and Dad would leave immediately, not caring about the time.

One fine Sunday, in the middle of the night, Dad was sleeping peacefully. Everything was quiet outside the house. Even the tree leaves weren't waving due to the lack of wind. The block of quarters was dark and only illuminated when a train passed by. Suddenly, someone banged on the door, twice, and called, "Mr. Pantoji, It's an emergency". Mom was startled and woke up in a panic. Dad got up yawning and went to open the door.

"Sir, it's an emergency at Loni station. You are asked to come in 15 minutes. Station Master is halting the next express train for you," said the man from Dad's office.

Dad let the information sink in for a moment and immediately went to get ready. Mom, who had calmed herself down was now sitting on the bed. This wasn't the first time that someone banged the door asking Dad to get ready at any time during the day or night.

My father had learned the art of getting ready in 10 minutes while my mother had gained expertise in preparing his lunch box in the same amount of time. And that tiffin included rotis and sabji and pickle. But when Dad had to run in no time, she would ask at which station he would be at lunchtime. She would then prepare the lunch box and go to the station. Everyone knew who she was. She would give that tiffin to the guard of the train headed to where Dad was working and the guard would then hand over the tiffin to my Dad. The same thing Grandma had done for years.

The man was waiting outside for my father. "I will be late," Dad informed Mom and left with the man to the station. Usually, express trains did not have a halt at kedgaon as it was a small town. But in case of emergency, the Station Master would make an exception by communicating to the driver to make a quick stop and let the S&T expert board the train. Because no other train could possibly reach the emergency spot quicker than the priority express trains.

When Dad reached the station, the train was in the vicinity of the platform. The Station Master made an entry of the halt when the train stopped at the platform. Dad and two more teammates boarded the train which immediately departed to the destination.

In just 20 minutes, the train arrived at Loni station. The team got off the train and headed quickly to the relay room. Usually, the panel in the cabin would show some kind of message about the failure in signaling. But Dad could not see any such error indication. The team already present in the relay room walked my father and his team through the procedure they had performed so far.

After checking regular circuits, Dad said, "It's a home signal failure. We have to inform Loni Station Master." The cabin man contacted the Station Master from the auto-phone from his cabin, "Sir, we have to halt upcoming trains." The cabin man checked the code sheet of trains and marked the trains that were due in the next 2 hours. The Station Master marked the codes of those trains on his sheet and contacted the Station Masters of the towns adjacent to Loni.

As it was a home signal failure, the S&T department cannot guarantee train safety. In such cases, the Station Master has to stop the trains from entering the station. Dad took out his Multimeter and followed the regular procedure to find the error. His team monitored the line to get a clear signal but nothing was happening. Dad didn't have much time as the whole schedule of the train was collapsing.

After a while, Senior Signal Engineers arrived at the relay room to find the base of the error. Between them was a 50-year-old man. The man had joined the S&T department after the death of his father. Under the scheme of the Indian railways, if an employee dies before retirement, the railway offers the job to the employee's son/daughter/wife. The man was just 18 when his father died. He joined the railways to earn money and feed his family. He couldn't even complete his graduation. This

50-year-old man was standing with a team of two senior engineers, a few signaling technicians including my Dad, and cabin men.

When every other professional present in the relay room was taking a guess about the error, the man confidently talked with his bold husky voice, "Sir," he said removing his cap and running his palm on his bald head. "The error is in the lower point...here," he pointed to the circuit and confidently spoke out his observation, "this particular condenser seems faulty."

The whole team traced the circuit the man was suggesting and there it was, a circuit failure. "Excellent Haridas," the Senior Engineer patted the man's shoulder.

Dad looked at the man in surprise. The whole team of professionals couldn't find the complicated failure that he had casually pointed out. Fortunately, the team fixed the circuit and trains started moving again.

The night had rested and the Sun brought beautiful colors to the sky. Dad and his team were preparing reports of the failure in the cabin. The Station Master from the night shift had gone home and the one from the day shift had arrived. Dad had seen people changing as the clock ticked to the end of the shift while he was still working. It didn't matter to him anymore what time it was and how long he hadn't eaten anything.

Dad and one of his teammates from Loni station, Mr. Ahuja finished the report while the rest of the team headed back to their respective work. It was 11 in the morning when Dad submitted the report. He had to stay at Loni for another 4 to 5 hours for the second round of inspection.

"Want to go out for a bite?" asked Mr. Ahuja. "There is a good diner down the street behind the station."

When Dad was about to reply, the next train arrived at the platform and he grinned, "My lunch is here."

Mr. Ahuja was confused but decided to follow his fellow teammate to the guard's compartment at the end of the train. Dad saw the guard holding a tiffin box on which 'MR. PANTOJI' was written in bold letters with nail polish.

Dad took the lunch box, thanked the guard, and went back to the office. "Come on," he said to Mr. Ahuja, "Let's have lunch."

When they reached the cabin, Dad and his colleague sat across the desk where Dad unpacked the lunch box.

"When did guard start the tiffin business?" chuckled Mr. Ahuja.

Dad laughed and replied, "My wife sent this." He knew she would have sent extra rotis. There were paper dishes in the office cupboard. He took out two and served Roti, potato sabji, salad, and pickle. Both of them were enjoying lunch in peace as the major error was solved, the report was done and they had good 4 hours left for the next inspection round.

"How did we miss the failure?" said Mr. Ahuja, grabbing a bite of the salad.

"It was a critical one," Dad replied, "By the way who that man was? It was as if he came to rescue us."

"Who? Haridas?" Mr. Ahuja asked, still enjoying the meal sent by my mother. "He is a gem for our department. Our boss trusts his instincts."

"I was surprised how casually, by just observing the circuit, he found the error."

"He is a good lad. Man lost his father to a heart attack when he was 18. He joined the department through the scheme. I heard he could not even complete his 12th grade as he had to financially support his family. But he helped his brothers get a good education. He also paid for their marriages while he decided not to get married himself. Every time he arrives, take a glance at the relay room and make suggestions. Always works. Solid experience."

Dad was quietly listening about the man who he thought was no less than a magician and prompted, "Sometimes, education doesn't define a man's work. Haridas is a living example of tremendous knowledge and experience."

CHAPTER TWENTY-THREE

THE FIRST GRANDCHILD

Every department in the Railways has to perform certain rounds of inspection every month. An officer/Engineer from various departments conducts both day and night inspection rounds in a month to re-assure the functioning of each piece of equipment. Walking in the tracks, through the ballast stones isn't easy, especially during night hours.

Sometimes, thieves would make their way to the standing train to steal whatever they could get. They would hide behind the bushes to wait for the goods train carrying petrol or diesel to pass by. Whenever the goods train had a long halt in the yard, these thieves would fill large containers with fuel. In the case of passenger trains, they would climb the window and steal the purses of women or injure passengers. And if they fail to grab anything, they would just throw stones at the train to irritate passengers. Railway Police Force immediately rush to handle such scenarios. They even patrol the trains to instruct passengers on closing the windows and keeping their luggage safe. These cases happen around the least crowded areas of railway tracks, usually away from residential areas.

One such night, my father and his team were inspecting the signals and tracks in Kedgaon and a few nearby stations. One passenger train was standing in the yard, waiting for the safe signal. Seeing a train full of passengers was a golden opportunity for the thieves. They started throwing stones to disturb passengers on board.

Out of nowhere, a pointy, fast-approaching stone bumped onto my father's forehead. A strong pain burst through his body and a blood drop rolled down his face. He froze for a moment, exhaling deeply. Inches of difference, and it could have been his eye.

"Sir, I think we should take you to the office," said Dad's colleague.

"No." Dad firmly replied, "The work must go on." And they completed the inspection. He never liked taking a sick leave or any small reason to get away from work.

He pressed his handkerchief on the wound to stop the blood flow. That morning, he reached home early, only to get back on duty in an hour. Mom quickly put a band-aid on his forehead from the first aid kit before he rushed back to work.

In that hurry, he realized that it was about time Mom needed someone by her side all the time. He decided to send her to her parent's house so she could spend some time with her family and deliver the baby under the care of her mother. Nanna was transferred from Madha to Solapur in 1990. He had a comfortable house in Solapur city. The neighbourhood had a good hospital nearby. Dad knew that was the only place where his wife won't be alone and she will be happy to be around her siblings.

Nanna and Nanni came to Kedgaon to pick up their daughter. She packed her bag and had a last glance around the kitchen to make sure there was enough grocery for the next month.

At the station, Dad made sure she gets a window seat on the train. Mom was happy that she was going to spend the next few weeks with her parents. At the same time, she was sad to leave her students on their own until she returns.

The day before going to Solapur, she called all her students. As usual, she offered them cookies and revealed her plans.

"I will be away for a few weeks," she politely informed them. "But when I return, I will cover all the pending studies you have for the semester, okay?"

Kids nodded and agreed with their favorite teacher. They knew she would catch up with their syllabus whenever she returns. Mom assigned homework to each one of them for the whole next month. They promised they would finish all the homework.

Some of the girls among the students waited after the last class of the day to spend time with their teacher. Those sweet little girls were so fond of my mother that they felt the unborn child was no less than their sibling. Mom loved how those girls talked to her about their new dolls and dresses and started dreaming about her own daughter.

She was going to miss her students a lot. But now, she needed to focus on herself and her child. Nanna and Nanni took her to the station where Dad was holding the reservation ticket to the train. Mom carefully stepped inside the train compartment and watched Nanna tuck the luggage under the seat. Making herself comfortable at the window seat, she said to Dad, "There is a box of cookies on the shelf, have it with tea. Kitchen is pretty much stocked up. Don't burn the roti," she chuckled.

"Don't worry about me. I'll be fine. You take care of yourself," Dad smiled. He was standing on the platform till the train departed. Nanna promised my Dad to keep him posted on Mom's health. As the train went out of the vicinity, he imagined the empty house. For the next few weeks, he was going to be alone.

~~

"Are you comfortable?" Nanni asked her daughter who was enjoying the view from the train. Mom saw a beautiful river when the train passed over the bridge blowing the whistle, it calmed her mind.

"Yes. I am fine, mother," replied my Mom smiling at her mother. Nanni had prepared the meal for Dad as well as for the three of them to eat during the journey. She took out the tiffin and served three lunch plates. Mom was eating lunch with her parents after a long time. She and Nanna talked about her students. Nanni told her everything that was going on in Solapur and in their lives.

When they reached home, aunt Asha was waiting at the gate for her sister. Mom waved at her from the corner of the lane. Aunt Asha and uncle Avi immediately rushed to take the luggage. Mom was happy to see her siblings waiting for her like they always did. She had a special bond with her siblings. Her little sister and brother never took any decision without asking her opinion. Uncle Avi was a handsome young boy for whom his two sisters were everything. Aunt Asha, who was a sweet shy girl and had an even sweeter voice always treated my Mom as her second mother.

Mom went inside the house and took a seat on the chair next to the balcony. Aunt Asha had cleaned up the balcony for her elder sister. She had even set up a bed for Mom, closer to the kitchen so Mom could sneak around for her food cravings.

"Asha, you did this all by yourself?" Mom asked her little sister.

"Avi helped me. He has even brought your favorite sweet dishes this morning."

"Really? What have you got Avi?" she asked.

"Loads of sweets, Anju tai," he replied and rushed to the kitchen. In a couple of minutes, he came out holding a plate full of Motichoor Laddu, Barfi, and more sweets. Mom, who had craved only sweet dishes in her pregnancy took a hand full of Laddu and fed it to her siblings first. All three of Nanna's children spent hours in the balcony; giggling, talking, and teasing each other.

~~

At Nanna's, Mom was enjoying all the pampering she was getting from her family. She even went to a movie with her siblings, for old times' sake. The week passed quickly, waiting for her due date.

On the afternoon of 8th July 1990, Mom started experiencing labor pains. Nanni was busy cooking lunch in the kitchen. Uncle Avi was working on his project while Aunt Asha was practicing her singing.

"Mother, I think it's time," Mom said, calmly sitting on her bed.

Nanni panicked and rushed to her daughter. Uncle Avi hurried to the hospital already. The hospital was only a 10 minutes walk from the house. As Nanna wasn't home, uncle Avi returned with a taxi and called out to his sister, "Let's go. I have informed the hospital that we are coming."

The time between getting into the taxi, going into the pregnancy ward, and delivering a baby went so fast for Mom that the next thing she remembers was the nurse's words, "It's a girl." Holding the baby for the first time, she forgot all the pain and screams. The baby was healthy. Mom could see her nose on the baby and Dad's face line. She held the baby girl closer to her chest until the nurse took the child for the first bath.

Mom was sleeping when Nanna arrived in the room. He was looking at a little girl sleeping peacefully next to her mother in the crib. Mom slowly woke up and saw Nanna swinging the crib gently and affectionately looking at the newborn.

"How are you feeling?" Nanna asked his daughter with concern.

"A little tired," she replied looking at her daughter who was enjoying the little swings of a crib.

"I have called Anand from the office. He is stuck at work as usual. But he said he will take the first train to Solapur after his work."

Mom nodded and didn't complain as she was aware of Dad's duty. Instead, she focused on her daughter who seemed hungry now. Nanna left her alone with the child.

Dad visited the hospital the next morning, desperately waiting to see his daughter. He rushed to the room number told by the receptionist of the hospital. When Dad entered the room, he immediately saw his little daughter curled up on Mom's lap. Her tiny hands were tucked in a warm blanket.

"How's my little daughter and her mother?" he asked sitting in a chair next to his wife. When he settled, Mom carefully let him hold the baby in his lap. Glancing at the baby, he asked, "What should we call her?"

"I haven't thought of a name yet. What do you have in mind?" Mom giggled, observing how he was carefully holding the little baby.

"Well," he looked up at his wife and said, "I have been thinking about the name since I received the news."

"So? What's her name then?" Mom curiously asked.

"She is..." Dad held the baby close to his heart. "Aditi."

"Aditi," grinned my Mom "Beautiful name."

Dad looked at the child. Aditi was looking at him with little round eyes. He smiled at her, "Hey Aditi." The baby, who was meeting her Dad for the first time, curled up the corner of her lips and a cute little dimple appeared on her cheek.

"Look, she has a dimple like you," Mom giggled. Dad's dimples were different and were on both of his cheeks. The baby had inherited only one dimple on the right cheek, which was cuter.

My sister Aditi was a crybaby. She would cry whenever Mom was about to take a nap. She knew only two feelings in the world, crying and being hungry. Apart from these two, she didn't like anything else. She would cry so much that aunt Asha and uncle Avi would leave for the college yawning, with puffy red eyes. My sister had earned expertise in crying the whole night and then sleeping all day long. She was messing up the whole schedule. If at all, on rare occasions, when she won't cry, Nanni would tease Mom, "How come she is quiet?"

That month and a half that Mom and the baby spent at Nanna's was wonderful for all of them. No matter how much the baby cried, they all loved Aditi. They loved the smell of baby powder and oil and even of the baby's potty. It was all cute and the day would go fast in taking care of the baby. One day they realized, the baby stops crying when uncle Avi held her close to his heart.

"She loves her uncle," uncle Avi would brag. From that day, he was in charge of taking care of the baby when she cried, which was pretty much always. He loved how much his little niece felt secure and warm in his arms. The baby was the center of attraction in the family. During the time when Mom and the baby were at Nanna's; Dad, Grandpa, and Grandma often visited to meet little Aditi. The whole environment of the house changed with the arrival of my sister, Pantoji's first grandchild.

CHAPTER TWENTY-FOUR

A New Little Member of a Family

"She is so tiny," giggled Amol, the neighbour's son. Mom had returned to Kedgaon when Aditi was 6 weeks old. Nanni insisted she stay for another month, but Mom's life in Kedgaon was calling her. Dad went to pick up his little daughter and wife. He brought the crib along to set it up next to the bed in the railway quarter. Aditi was sleeping in the crib when Mrs. Patil and her children came to see the new baby.

"Because she is just a month and a half old," said Mrs. Patil to Amol. He was curious to see the child and was wondering if he looked the same when he was small. Mrs. Patil had knitted a wool blanket and sweater for Mom's first child, which she brought with her as a gift.

"I hope it will fit her," Mrs. Patil said looking at a baby girl who was waking up from her long nap.

"Why don't you try it on her? She is awake," Mom carefully picked up Aditi from the crib. She let Aditi come back to reality and nodded at Mrs. Patil. Mrs. Patil then took the baby in her lap and widely grinned. Aditi, as usual, identified the unfamiliar lap and started crying. Mrs. Patil held her close and patted her back for a few minutes. And she stopped crying. It was a miracle only uncle Avi was able to do. Mrs. Patil brushed her fingertips on baby's cheeks and forehead, "She is so sweet." She then tried the new sweater on Aditi, which fit perfectly. The sleeves were a little longer, but Mrs. Patil folded the sleeves and made them comfortable for the baby. Aditi seemed to like the sweater as she felt warm and a dimple appeared on her cheek as she smiled.

Mrs. Patil was experienced in taking care of a child. She had two of her own and claimed to have helped her sister in child nursing. She told my Mom that she has a special oil for baby massages and she gives an amazing bath to babies. Mom agreed as she trusted the woman in front of her. "I will get you warm fresh cow milk for breakfast and baby oil for Aditi's bath. Be right back," Mrs. Patil said.

Mom saw the woman rush to her home. She was happy to be in her own house, her own neighbourhood. She had missed that place and more importantly, her students. A thought of resuming classes peeked into her head. But now she had a baby to look after. Mom looked at her daughter and smiled. Aditi smiled back, and Mom felt immense happiness. She picked up the baby and headed to the bathroom when Mrs. Patil returned, excited to bathe my sister.

"Anjali, you enjoy this warm milk. I will massage the baby. Massage helps babies grow faster and their muscles get stronger."

Mom took a glass of warm milk from her and watched as Mrs. Patil started giving a soft yet professional baby massage. Aditi liked how Mrs. Patil was stroking her arms, legs, giving them a little stretch. She seemed to relax. Mrs. Patil then washed the oil from Aditi's body with gentle soap and warm water. Mom watched how easily Mrs. Patil was handling the baby. She wasn't rough, but not too soft either. It reflected her experience with the babies. Aditi went back to sleep immediately after a warm and soothing bath.

"Thank You, Mrs. Patil," Mom gently squeezed the neighbour's hand showing how grateful she was.

"It's my pleasure." Mrs. Patil lightly motioned the crib as she saw the baby's movements. "Besides, Aditi enjoyed it. Call me anytime you need okay?" she said and left the house saying, "You should take a nap too."

That day, Dad came home early with a lot of comfortable clothes and some soft toys for the baby. Mom cooked dinner in her own kitchen after so long. Both of them enjoyed Mom's special Masala Rice together. This time, baby Aditi was accompanying them. Dad wasn't paying attention to what Mom was talking about. He was constantly looking at the baby. The father inside him was more biased towards the baby now.

The next day, as usual, Mom prepared a lunch box for Dad. He was going to be away for the day, so he requested Mrs. Patil if she could stay with his wife and daughter. She agreed and said reassuringly, "Don't worry. I'm happy to help."

Mom and Mrs. Patil were sitting and talking in the front yard about the town, neighbours, and new recipes. Suddenly, a distant voice of children giggling reached their ears. Mom looked in the direction of the voice and saw her students approaching, almost running towards her.

"Madam," one of them said, "we are here to see the baby." Mom saw all her students gathering around the front yard. She was pleased to see them again. She brought Aditi out in the front yard from the crib and instead of directly showing her to the students, she placed her carefully in Mrs. Patil's lap. She knew Mrs. Patil would not let kids touch the baby and be careful with her daughter.

Children gathered around. Some of them held their finger near the baby, which Aditi grabbed in her tiny palms. Some tried to pull her cheeks, but Mrs. Patil widened her eyes at them, "No touching. She is sensitive. Babies catch allergies quite easily."

Mom was sitting in a chair, looking at all the children who had accompanied her during pregnancy. She brought out a carpet and asked them to take a seat. Students sat down giggling and muttering about the new member of the family. She brought out some cookies served on a large plate and placed them at the center of the carpet. The plate was empty within a minute.

"So," Mom started talking to them, "how is your study going?"

"We completed the homework you had given us before leaving," said one of the girls, and everybody nodded. Mom was glad that they genuinely finished the studies she had asked for.

"That's really nice. And how were your results for the final exam?"

Everyone told their grades and marks one by one to their favorite teacher who was proud to hear how well they had scored. She knew they would perform amazingly in the exam. She was worried about Mayur, who wasn't there with all the students.

"Mayur didn't come?" she asked.

"I'm here...I'm here," came the voice and Mom saw little Mayur rushing towards her carrying a scorecard in his hand. "Sorry Madam, I am late. I was finishing the homework," said the boy, catching his breath, and sat down on the carpet. He then handed the scorecard to my Mom, "See Madam, my final exam results."

Mom scanned the document carefully. "Wonderful," she expressed, "Fantastic, Mayur. Congratulations. I am proud of you," said my mother to the boy who couldn't read a few months ago but now had scored good marks in all subjects.

"You all scored really well." Mom clapped for them and the kids clapped along. "We should have another round of cookies." Kids cheered enthusiastically. Mom brought out more cookies and this time too, the kids finished the plate quickly. Grinning at each other, they took bites of the cookies and celebrated their exam results.

Mom spent some more time with the students. "I will have to reschedule the batches. Meet me the day after tomorrow at the same time, I will tell you the new timings of your batches, okay?"

"Okay," the kids replied in harmony.

Mom saw her students run away to the playground as she took Aditi inside the house. She could see the progress in the way they talked and carried themselves confidently.

Mrs. Patil was being supportive and was generously helping my mother. Grandpa and Grandma would sometimes stay for a night or two in the town to spend time with their first granddaughter. Mr. and Mrs. Gokhale were regular visitors to play with the little girl.

Mom rescheduled the coaching classes as per Aditi's sleep and food timings. Students happily accepted the new timetable, and everything was back to where it was left. Now her coaching classes, a big family of students, had a new little member.

CHAPTER TWENTY-FIVE

DAD'S THREE AWARDS

"Bye Dad. Come home soon," little Aditi hugged her father as he was leaving for work. Dad was now trying his best to manage his daughter's demands and work schedule. He enjoyed new responsibilities on him at work as well as at home. Now that he was getting even better at understanding the signaling errors, he could quickly solve the problems. However, temporary solutions weren't the best choice, he wanted to fix the commonly occurring errors once and for all.

After thoroughly studying the last records of failures, he came up with a few techniques to reduce those errors. Finally, he had a full-fledged report ready to share with his colleagues.

"It's simple, we need to do periodical servicing of each piece of equipment," Dad said to his team. "According to my observation, this is what I think should be the time interval between two servicing routines. So, the current interval is a bit longer. By reducing the timestamp between two routines, I am sure we can reduce the failures." Dad showed the reports to his team and all of them worked on the new solution to give it a shot. Eventually, the failure rate was considerably reduced. Dad's superiors were very happy to see the result.

Meanwhile, at home, my sister was growing up with all the students in Mom's coaching classes. She was a year old when she started listening to the lectures. Years passed as she began her school life and studied along with the rest of the students. Mom never treated her any special. During classes, little Aditi was a student.

It was the year 1996 when my Mom was pregnant for the second time. Little Aditi was 6 years old. She still was a crybaby. But her sleep schedule was sorted as she had to wake up early to go to school. She would deny going anywhere without either of her parents by faking stomachaches and headaches. But Mom knew when she was lying and when her stomach was really hurting.

Seeing Mom's belly she would ask thousands of questions. "It's your sibling," Mom would answer. "Very soon, we are going to have a baby in our family." Aditi would get curious and wonder if the little baby would look like one of her dolls.

Dad was busy managing the signaling in his section, he was meeting a lot of people. Technicians would come to him for solutions regarding signal or track point errors. He was working day and night. People would say, "Anand is like his father, hardworking, smart, and humble." Grandpa was hearing about Dad's work from his friends and was proud to see his son succeeding in the department.

One day, Dad was on the field for regular inspection of all the signals and gates. He had checked the relay room before leaving for the inspection and had found no error. It was just a regular check-up of the working of the equipment alongside the tracks. As he was noting down the points in his journal to prepare the report, he saw a team of officers heading his way. One of them waved at him and he understood who all of them were. It was the Senior Divisional Signal and Telecom Engineer (Sr. DSTE). He was there to inspect Dad's work and the overall section. His team had top Signal Inspectors from various sections of the Central Railways. Dad wasn't expecting them, but he had to be prepared.

"Mr. Pantoji, right?" asked senior DSTE.

"Yes, Sir," Dad replied, closing his register and adjusting his posture in front of his superiors.

"Nice to meet you, Mr. Pantoji," he greeted and asked, "May I see your file?"

Dad handed over the register to one of the teammates of senior DSTE and confidently waited for him to have a glance at it.

"We have heard a lot about you. You seem to have reduced the signaling errors in this area."

"Sir," My father began explaining his work, "I have been monitoring common errors and trying to find a permanent or at least a long-lasting solution. Some of them are still under observation and some are working as per my expectations, sir. I can show you the report and changes in the relay room as well."

Officers muttered something in between themselves and one of them curiously said, "We would like to see the reports."

"This way, sir," my father led the team towards his cabin. They all followed him and watched how comfortable he was with them. He was answering every question confidently. When they reached Dad's cabin, he pulled out a detailed report along with circuit diagrams from his desk drawer and handed it over to the team.

They all sat across Dad's table and started reading the report. Meanwhile, Dad quickly ordered some ginger tea for all of them from his desk telephone. When the officers were taking notes on my father's reports, senior DSTE was asking tons of questions about Dad's plans regarding the work. Dad answered every question in detail and explained how he came up with the solution.

"The report is very thorough, I must say," said one of the inspectors. Dad explained the parts where he thought the solution would work even in worst-case scenarios. When the office boy returned with tea, Dad asked the Sr. DSTE and his team to be comfortable and enjoy the tea.

Dad then talked about some more solutions he had in mind to optimize electromechanical signals in his work radius. The surprise visit of senior DSTE and his team to check my father's work had gone really well. Dad was satisfied that he could explain what he has been working on for more than 4 years now.

He thought it was the best day of his career since he joined the Indian Central Railways. But the best was yet to come.

~~

In India, spending the last month of pregnancy with parents is quite a tradition. Women feel secure with their mothers. For her second pregnancy, Mom again went to Nanna's house as the hospital in Solapur was comfortable and good.

Aditi was missing her father and would cry to call him at work. He would take a train to Solapur to meet his daughter and go back to work. Little Aditi wanted both of her parents to be with her all the time.

Nanni tried to explain to her, "Your little brother or sister will be here in a week, okay?" Aditi nodded anxiously, wondering why that was connected to her and Mom living at Nanna's house. "Your Mom needs good rest and all the care she gets. And more importantly, she needs my help, okay? So for a few days, you have to live here."

"But I want to go back. Dad is alone there."

"Your father is not alone. He has a lot of work to do and he's got friends as you do," Nanni assured her granddaughter, "You were born here too. Now it's your sibling who wants his big sister Aditi to stay here."

Eventually, she agreed but twice a day she would cry to meet Dad. Dad tried his best to balance work and his daughter's demands.

It was the 8th of September 1996. Dad had received a letter from senior DSTE to appreciate his work. Department liked his solution to reduce failures. When Dad was reading the letter sitting in his cabin, the landline on his desk rang.

"Hello?" he said, still focused on the letter.

"Anjali has gone into labor, can you come here today?" it was uncle Avi on the other side of the phone.

"When? How is she?"

"This morning, she is fine."

"Alright, I will be there," Dad hung up the call. Abandoning the letter in his hand, he quickly left the cabin to take permission to leave the town, which took a lot of time. Finally, he boarded the last train and hurried to the hospital as soon as the train arrived at the Solapur platform. In all this rush, he couldn't finish reading the letter from Senior DSTE. The letter was still on his desk.

When he reached the hospital, he saw Nanna and uncle Avi sitting in the hospital lobby.

"We were waiting for you," said Nanna, brightly smiling, "Congratulations, Anand."

"Is she alright? How is the baby?" Dad asked with concern. "Yes. Both of them are perfectly healthy," uncle Avi told him the room number and Dad rushed to the pregnancy ward.

As he entered the room, he saw little Aditi sitting next to Mom. He followed her gaze, and there, on Mom's lap was me, another daughter. Dad grinned and came closer to see the baby. This time, the baby had Mom's face, about which she bragged. Dad picked me up and held me closer. Pulling Aditi onto his lap, he hugged his two adorable daughters.

"Dad, she is my sister," said little Aditi. "Mom says I am her big sister so I have to take care of her."

Dad smiled and said, "Yeah, you are a big sister now."

Aditi seemed confused and to be honest, a little pissed at me as she now had to share her parents with me. I, on the other hand, was happy to sleep all the time. I wasn't a crybaby. I had a baby routine. I would sleep on time, drink milk on time, and didn't ruin anyone's sleep schedule. Of course, I would cry when I was hungry or needed attention, but uncle Avi would hug me and I would stop crying right away. Uncle Avi had some sort of miracle in his hug, it was his love for his nieces.

When I was curled up in Dad's arms in the hospital on the day of my birth, the reception of the hospital received a call. The receptionist came to Mom's room and asked, "Anand Pantoji? We have a call for you at reception. Would you come to the front desk?"

Dad asked if he can take the baby along with him. Mom nodded and handed him a baby blanket. He tucked the warm blanket around me and headed to the reception holding me in his arms.

"Hello, this is Anand," he said on the phone receiver.

"Anand, it's me. Mr. Gokhale."

"Oh, hello uncle. Did you hear the news? I'm blessed with another daughter," Dad grinned, looking at the baby in his arms.

"Really? That's amazing. Congratulations my son," Mr. Gokhale replied enthusiastically and continued, "There is something you need to know."

"What is it?"

"Your new baby has brought good vibes I bet," he replied, "Did you read the whole letter from senior DSTE?"

"Umm...I guess not. I was reading it but then I had to be here...," Dad replied, trying to remember the letter.

"Well, congratulations Anand, you have won Divisional Railway Award for your amazing work."

"What?" Dad could not believe it. It was his first award. He had worked day and night to keep the trains working and signals functioning. He didn't say anything. He just looked at me and smiled.

"The award ceremony is in Solapur Divisional office in two weeks." Mr. Gokhale informed and congratulated Dad on the award as well as the new baby's arrival.

Dad went back to Mom's room in the hospital and saw Grandpa and Grandma sitting on the sofa in the room.

"Anand, where is my granddaughter," Grandma cheerfully asked. Dad handed me to Grandma's lap. Grandma had wished for a grandson. But I had plans to become a good daughter like my sister.

"Now she looks more like Anjali," Grandma said, taking a good look at me.

"No, she looks like me," argued little Aditi, and everyone laughed, agreeing with her.

"What the call was about?" Mom asked as Dad settled down next to her on a chair. Dad grinned and said, "Our little baby has brought good fortune with her. I have won an award for my work." He disclosed the news to everyone. Grandpa was so happy that tears rolled down his cheeks. He hugged my father and said, "I am proud of you, son."

Mom was happy hearing about her husband's success and the reward he got for it. She had seen him work under pressure when a major failure occurred in the middle of the night. She had witnessed abrupt work calls and watched him rush to the station without completing his lunch. She was a proud wife, and now a mother of two beautiful daughters.

That day, Nanni cooked delicious food to celebrate Dad's award and my arrival into the family. Dad was sitting next to my crib.

"So, what are you going to call her?" asked Nanni to both Mom and Dad.

"This time, Anjali will decide the Name. I got that chance when I named Aditi," said my Dad looking at his wife who now was thinking about a good name.

"I like short names," said Mom. "Umm....mother, what was that name you suggested? Something about lyrics in *Rigveda*?"

Nanni thought for a moment and remembered what name she had recommended a few days ago, "Rucha?"

"Rucha, yes," grinned my mother. "We will call her Rucha."

"It's a beautiful Name. I love it," Dad looked at me. Little Rucha was sleeping peacefully.

"Anand, how do you feel?" asked Nanna to his son-in-law.

"Today, I won an award. Now I have three of them," Dad proudly replied looking at both of his daughters.

KEDGAON TOWN FADED IN THE BACKGROUND

The Moment when Dad received his first award was glorious and cheerful. The audience sitting in the hall was applauding loudly when he walked up to the stage. Many railway engineers from different sections in the Solapur division received an award that day.

Mom and I could not attend the award function as I was only two weeks old. But Nanna, Grandpa, Grandma, and Aditi went to see him collect that beautiful golden shield crafted with words: Divisional Railway Award for Excellent work.

When Dad returned home to show the shield to everybody, I was playing with the musical toy hanging on the upper handle of my crib. He picked me up on his lap. Aditi wandered into the house to find Nanni. Her search ended in the kitchen where Nanni was making chocolate milk for her.

"I think I might get promoted," Dad told his wife as she was listening to the award ceremony from Nanna.

"Really?" Mom grinned with pride and said, "You deserve it."

"Yes, but I might get transferred as well. So we might have to leave kedgaon," Dad informed her with a heavy heart. He was aware of Mom's affection towards her coaching classes and Kedgaon.

"It's alright. Wherever it is, we will adjust," she assured him. Deep down, she was a bit worried and wondered in which town we all might end up. She knew that the promotion comes with a transfer order in the majority of the cases. Keeping a smile on her face to hide her concern, "Don't worry, we will settle in the new town as we did in Kedgaon," she said thoughtfully.

But Dad had the whole thing planned. Before my sister and I, Mom was the only one living in that railway quarter. Mom had a difficult time in that home in her initial days. Even though she got used to staying alone without electricity, walking to the water-well to fill the buckets when the tap water didn't work, and constantly worrying about snakes and lizards, Dad wanted her to have a comfortable life now. Besides, he now had two little girls to look after.

"No matter where I get transferred, you and the kids will stay in Daund, with my parents," Dad announced his decision. "I don't want you or the girls to suffer because of my job."

"But what about you? How will you manage alone?" Mom asked with concern. "Besides, Aditi won't let you go. And Rucha will miss her Dad's warmth in the house."

"I know. I understand, but this is for the best. Kids will stay in Daund and will complete their education. It's not easy for kids to change schools, you know. It takes time to adjust. Let's not do that to our daughters"

Mom nodded. She thought about it and realized now both of them had to make decisions in their kid's favor.

~~

Mom, Aditi, and I returned to kedgaon the next week. Mrs. Patil, as expected, visited to see the new baby. She had knitted a soft and warm woolen blanket and sweater for me as she did for Aditi. She gave me her special massage and bath. She almost repeated everything she did for Aditi with me. Now it was my turn to enjoy all that pampering.

Now I was the center of attraction. Mom's students came to see me. They held fingers for me to grab. And as I used to sleep at regular times, Mom didn't have to change her schedule for me.

"She is anti-Aditi," Grandma would tease.

Aditi, who occasionally hated that everyone was taking care of me, would say weird things to Grandma like, "Why don't you take the baby with you? The baby is staying with us for so long. And she sleeps in Mom's lap. Where will I sleep then?" Grandma would laugh and explain to her, "She is your sister. We cannot take her with us."

Sometimes, if Aditi felt she was not getting enough attention, she would talk about herself in the third person, "Mom, she is hungry." or "Mom, she needs to sleep now." Mom would try to correct her narrative but it was easier to pay her some attention.

No matter how dramatic my sister was, she loved me. She would sometimes feed me water by spoon and grin when I drank it without crying or choking. It was all fun for her. She would tell her friends, "There is a baby staying in our home. She is my sister." And her friends would come to see me after school. Sometimes, students from the coaching classes would stay longer to play with me. The older students even took care of me if Mom needed to go out for a couple of minutes. As now Mom couldn't drop Aditi at her school, the neighbour's children would take her with them to school on their cycles. Aditi enjoyed those cycle rides. The entire Kedgaon town was a big family where people helped each other.

One day, Mom called the parents of all her students to inform them that she would no longer be able to take classes as she was moving to Daund.

"I might be leaving soon. My husband and I both think that Aditi and Rucha should complete their education in one city. So we decided, the kids and I shift to Daund. I won't be able to continue coaching classes. I am really sorry."

Some of the parents understood her situation, some insisted to stay, some said they are going to miss her, some parents were sad as their little ones were about to join Mom's coaching. But they eventually agreed. Mom was not ready to leave everything behind. But her priority was her children. She decided to stop her career to take care of Aditi and me. Daund was a comparatively more developed town than Kedgaon. Plenty of private coaching classes in every other neighbourhood. Mom knew she cannot have the same thing she had in Kedgaon.

In a week, Dad's transfer order arrived at his cabin. He opened the letter and read.

Previous position: Senior Signal Technician. Reporting Station: Kedgaon

New Position: Signal Engineer. Reporting Station: Daund.

The last word caught his attention. Daund! A wide grin spread over his face. He was now an Engineer and he was relieved to see the destination station as his hometown.

Daund always had a special place in his heart.

Dad came home early to inform Mom that they had to leave in two days for Daund.

"I have been transferred to Daund and promoted to an Engineer's position," he revealed the news.

"That is great," she smiled and said, "I am glad we all will be together."

For the next two days, Mom was packing bags. Mrs. Patil was helping her. Mom thought Aditi might miss her friends and school. Instead, anything to get a day off from school without pretending to be sick was a win-win for her.

"I will miss you Anjali, and the girls. I wish you didn't have to leave. But I understand," Mrs. Patil had tears in her eyes. For the past few years, she and Mom were good friends. They would go to the market together. Mom would call her for tea, she would call Mom for breakfast. She would bathe Aditi and me. Mom would teach her sons. Mrs. Patil was like an elder sister to my mother. Mr. Patil and my Dad were friends too, but they rarely had time to sit in the front yard and talk.

"I will miss you too. And I am grateful for everything you did for me and the girls." Mom hugged her and said, "You are always welcome to visit me in Daund."

Kedgaon town was welcoming and soothing. She was going to miss that house and the town. Mom's students kept visiting her for the next two days. They were not happy to see her leave the town. She had helped them get good scores in exams, she had told them stories, and gave them lots of cookies over the years. Mayur, who once was a scared little child, was now a confident smart student. He brought a rose flower for his teacher and said, "I will never forget your teaching and how much you helped me. Someday, I will get a good job and will bring you a saree."

That made my Mom's eyes wet with happiness. She had a life in that town, now it was all going to be just a part of her life that she had to leave behind.

The day arrived when Mom and Dad bid goodbye to everyone. Mom got the last plate of cookies for her students. She watched them eat the cookies and wave at her as she headed to the railway station with Aditi and little me.

As the train left the station, the Kedgaon town faded in the background.

CHAPTER TWENTY-SEVEN

THE ENGINE RIDE

No matter where you go in life, your childhood home remains special to you. Those memories. That invisible yet strong bond stays with you forever. Our house in Daund, with two bedrooms, a big kitchen, and a perfectly warm living room, was beautiful. In that very house, my sister and I were growing up. We would spend hours playing in the big front yard. In the backyard, Mom had enough space for gardening. The terrace of that house had witnessed how sincerely my sister and I would study. In the summer holidays, the terrace was our bedroom. We would sleep under the stars with the soothing breeze. It was perfect.

Those childhood days were wonderful. We made friends in the neighbourhood. We all would gather around in the evening to play cricket and hide & seek of our own rules.

Aditi and I were in the same school, near Daund railway station. But she was in 7th grade and I was in kindergarten. Our timings were different. I had to go to school at 8 in the morning, and she had her classes from 12 noon to 5 in the evening. Sometimes, Dad would drop me at school on his cycle. I would sit in the basket attached to his cycle. Mom would come to pick me up on her own cycle. If Aditi had her class timing synced with mine, which was rare, she would pick me up. I wanted my own cycle too, like the rest of my family. But I was too young. A few years later, Grandpa got me my first cycle on my birthday. My sister, our cousins, and I rode our cycles so carelessly that we often came home with wounded knees, yet we didn't stop roaming around in the town.

During the summer holidays, all my cousins would arrive to spend some time in Daund with us. Aunt Aruna's son Ojas and daughter Devashree, uncle Anil's son Siddharth, elder uncle Anupam's daughter Aishwarya, my sister, and I, we were a team of daemons. I was the youngest of all and would make sure all my big brothers and sisters are pampering me well. We all loved messing up the house, screaming, running around the neighbourhood, riding bicycles, and irritating our respective parents. Out of all of us, big brother Ojas was the most active and creative daemon. He had the guts to climb up the terrace from the water pipes or windows and jump down from the terrace to the floor. He was fearless. Brother Siddharth, on the other hand, was a bit shy, geeky humble boy. He would draw airplanes and trains all over the walls. He would take me on a bike ride and make drawings with me on our computer.

My sisters and I, we girls were good daemons. We would make *Rangolis* during the festival and brag about it. We had nothing to worry about.

Even though, we all children were kind of similar, especially siblings; my sister and I were totally different. We had nothing in common, no similarities, except our voice. Weirdly, we have identical voices. We could have pranked people using our little feature, but sadly, apart from answering each other's phone calls, we did nothing creative. Sometimes, even Mom and Dad get confused with our voices. But the rest of the things are so different between us that it's hard to tell we are sisters.

Aditi would talk very little and was mostly shy, I was talkative and didn't care what others will think. She was scared of most things and I was kind of brave, except for lizards and cockroaches. She was careful and I was annoying. She would study for hours, I would just complete homework in an hour. But we both got good scores every year.

We used to fight a lot and every time it was me who hit her and made her cry. We had all those siblings-conflicts. But we loved each other. Showing too much love to the siblings spoils them, so we kept our affection towards one another limited to a few occasions per year. Of course, we changed a lot over the years. Childhood was carefree and so were we.

During the Diwali Festival, Grandpa would call all his children and grandchildren to spend a few days with him at our house. All my cousin brothers and sisters would enjoy those festive holidays by eating sweets and burning firecrackers on the terrace. One day during the Diwali holidays, all my cousins, Aditi, and I were playing cards with Grandpa. Dad and the rest of the family were sitting in the living room watching us play.

"Uncle," said brother Ojas to my Dad, "Is it true what Grandpa said?"

"What did he say?"

"That you can take us to have a ride in the train engine. And we can even blow the horn?"

"Grandpa said that?" asked my Dad looking at Grandpa who was laughing. He did tell all of us that Dad was going to take us on an engine ride. And we were all very excited about it.

Dad had once taken Aditi on the engine and she was bragging about it. He looked at Ojas, trying to figure out what to say. But it was too late. We all were looking at him with our twinkly eyes in hope. He had to say yes.

Dad made a few phone calls to arrange our engine ride. Daund is a junction. Trains from almost every corner of India pass via Daund. Railway tracks in Daund have double lines. So, whenever a train had to change direction, the engine had to switch to the opposite end of the train. Daund was the station where the change of engine direction would take place for some trains. The whole process involved a good 15 minutes of engine ride on a track of around 1 km in length.

One express train was on its way to Daund from Pune, which needed to change the engine direction towards Manmad station. Dad took us all to the railway station. He had already contacted the driver who agreed to take the kids on board. While waiting near Dad's cabin, we saw the train arriving at the station. I started jumping in excitement. We all went near the engine and saw the driver waving at us from the side window. He was Dad's friend who smiled to see 6 little kids waiting curiously to get a ride in the engine. Dad and the driver carefully helped all of us board the engine. I was expecting steering in the driver's hands, but it was a big complicated machine with LEDs over some buttons. To be honest, I was disappointed at first, but it turned out to be super interesting and adventurous.

The driver explained to us how the track is already set to change the direction, he had to take the engine to the other end of the train. He described a lot about the working of the machine. I didn't understand a word he was saying. But I listened, curiously. The ride, indeed, was going wonderful.

He called me closer to his seat and asked, "Would you like to blow the horn?" I curiously nodded, something good was about to happen. He showed me the button and said, "Press this with the full force you have." And I wondered why do I need to apply full force to just press a small metal button. I understood soon when I tried to press it. It wasn't that easy. Dad held my finger and pressed the button. It was my finger but Dad's force and we all heard the horn blowing. I was so proud of myself.

The engine drove through the crossing and came back on the same track, in another direction of the train. We experienced a small thud when the engine got attached to the train. I had never been to the engine before and it was the best day of my life. I already felt like a young woman capable of driving the train engine. At that moment, I knew what I was going to write in my Diwali vacation essay, 'The day I rode the train engine."

The driver of the train had a small torch in his work bag. He took it out and gave it to me as a gift. "This is for excellent performance in train engine," he said to me. I looked at my Dad with a big smile. I kept that torch for years. I still remember how much fun we all children had on our first engine ride.

Back home, I told Grandpa everything that happened on the train engine. I bragged about it for so many years, just like my sister did.

I spent the next day writing an essay about it and showed it to my mother. She loved it and said, "You should definitely submit this homework."

After that, Dad took me and Aditi on an engine ride so many times. We even got to travel in the guard's compartment. Engine rides were always memorable. But the first one was my favorite.

CHAPTER TWENTY-EIGHT

THE MAN OF RAILWAYS

Graceful greenery and September rain were beautifying the whole town. My birthday was a week away and I had already given a list of gifts to my father. Almost every year, my birthday comes in between Ganesh Festival and that's something I love about September the most. I used to wait desperately for September to arrive. In school, I used to share chocolates with my friends on my birthday and invite them to the celebration at home. Mom used to make delicious food. Not to mention the *Prasad* for Ganesh Pooja. Everything was super exciting.

On my 7th birthday, I woke up with my sister whispering the 'Happy Birthday' song in my ear. I smiled and hugged her. Mom was already busy in the kitchen preparing delicious lunch. Grandma and Grandpa had brought Jalebi, my favorite sweet dish, and some snacks for the breakfast.

I got out of bed, quickly got ready, and wore a new dress that Grandpa had gifted me. Excited for the day, I went into the kitchen. "Happy Birthday Sweetie," Mom hugged me and patted me on my back. I returned the gesture with an even tighter hug. Then I ran to Grandpa and Grandma who both were sitting at the dining table, serving Jalebi and snacks in two plates for me and Aditi.

I touched their feet to take the blessing and sat down next to Grandpa. "Mom? Where is Dad? He hasn't returned yet?" I asked when I realized Dad had hurried to the office the last evening.

"No Sweetie. He is still working," Mom replied sauteing chopped potato in the pan. "But don't worry. He said he will be home for your birthday party."

"Okay." I smiled and shifted my whole focus to the delicious breakfast in front of me. "First pray to the god and then eat breakfast," Grandma ordered. Aditi and I went to the living room where we had decorated a corner to place Lord *Ganesha Murty* for the 10-day festival.

Both of us prayed to god and hurried back to the kitchen. Aditi finished her breakfast quickly and ran to the bedroom. She returned with a handmade birthday card for me. There was a drawing of two girls playing and a message saying 'Happy Birthday to my little and weird sister.' I loved it and gave a bone-crushing hug to my sister.

That day, my sister and I spent time watching our favorite cartoons till lunchtime. When a delicious aroma of potato Sabji and Puri hit my nose, I ran to the kitchen followed by my sister who quickly switched off the TV.

"Take a seat for the lunch, Girls. I am serving hot Puris." Aditi and I took a seat on the floor where a beautiful carpet and some flower decorations were waiting for us. Mom served two plates and started frying the Puris.

My sister and I thoroughly enjoyed the lunch while discussing who all were coming to my birthday party. My school friends, our friends from the neighbourhood, and some of Aditi's friends. I was excitedly waiting for the evening.

When the clock hit 5 in the evening, Aditi and Grandpa started arranging some balloons in the living room. While both of them were busy decorating the house, Mom was icing my birthday cake. And I was staring at the door every now and then, waiting for my Dad.

"Honey, your friends will arrive anytime now. Let's go get changed, okay?" Mom said putting the cake in the fridge. I nodded and followed her into the bedroom. A beautiful pink floral dress was kept on the bed. "Mom, I love the dress," I practically screamed with excitement.

"It's a gift from Dad and me," Mom smiled and helped me put the dress on. She then combed my hair and put a matching pink hairband over my head. It was beautiful. "I totally look like a Disney princess," I said glancing in the mirror with twinkly eyes. Mom laughed and replied with the same enthusiasm, "Yes sweetie. You do look like a princess."

At 6 in the evening, the living room was filled with all my friends. It was chaos that I was enjoying. My classmates complimented my dress. I couldn't stop smiling. "So, when are you going to cut the cake?" one of my friends asked, glancing at the mouth-watery cake on the table. "Just as soon as my Dad arrives," I replied looking at the front door. We waited for an hour, playing random games and entertaining our guests. But Dad was not even in proximity.

"Mom?" I called her impatiently, "You said Dad will be here for the party. Where is he?" I knew he was busy. But it was my birthday. I was mad at him for being late. "We will wait for another 10 minutes and then cut the cake." Mom assured me. "No. I won't cut the cake without him."

"Honey, all your friends are hungry. Dad will be here as soon as he can."

I nodded, not liking the plan. But Mom was right. My friends were hungry and so was I. After waiting for 10 minutes, we decided to cut the cake. All my friends gathered around to clap and cheer and sing the birthday song for me. We had snacks and chocolates and a lot of cake. Later, we all prayed to Lord Ganesha. All my friends gave me gifts and hugs and went back home.

Dinner was rather light and simple. Aditi and I finished the plate and went to watch TV. Dad still hadn't come home. I was wondering what was so important than my birthday that Dad had to miss the party. He went to the office the last evening, which was more than 24 hours ago. What made him stay out late on my birthday?

"It's bedtime," Mom called and we switched the TV off. I climbed onto the bed next to Aditi, and without saying anything or without arguing to watch more TV, decided to sleep. Mom switched the lights off and sat next to us until we were snoring.

In my dream, I was fighting with my Dad for not attending my birthday party and he was offering me a lot of candies. It was something around 2 in the morning when we all heard a knock on the door. Mom got up to open the door. I heard Dad talking to her about some complications at work and he had to stay. I got out of my bed, ready to fight with him.

"Hey little one," Dad pulled me over his lap and hugged me, "Happy Birthday."

"It was yesterday." I rolled my eyes at him, "My birthday was yesterday."

Dad looked at Mom who gave him an expression of 'I didn't miss her party, you did. Now handle her.' I could see Dad wondering what to say to me. He came up with the most obvious reply, "I am sorry sweetie. I was stuck at work. My boss was there too. I couldn't leave early."

"Did you tell your boss that it was my birthday and you can't miss it?"

"Well...," Dad again looked at Mom, asking for help. When she shrugged and pretended to be on my side, Dad replied gently, "I told my boss that it was your birthday. In fact, I invited him to the party. But the issue we were having at work was really big. It could have created an even bigger problem. So my boss and I decided to skip the party and rather buy you a big gift. How about that?"

I looked at Mom, she gave me an encouraging nod. After thinking for a few seconds, I decided to consider the offer. "Alright. I forgive you. But only if you eat cake with me and buy me ice cream tomorrow."

Dad laughed and nodded. Mom brought some cake and woke up my sister. We all enjoyed the late-night cake party. When I think about that night, I could see in my Dad's eyes that he wanted to be there for my birthday even more than I wanted him to be there. His work was critical and the work hours were uncertain. This used to happen a lot. Dad missed so many birthdays of his daughters. He missed a lot of festivals, especially Ganesh pooja. There hasn't been a festival where Dad was fully present. He either had to rush to work abruptly or completely miss the festival. We have spent a lot of important days without him. It had become a new normal. My sister and I used to get mad once in a while because everybody else's fathers used to be there for birthdays, school annual functions, parent-teacher meetings, and all festivals. Our Dad was always busy working. He prioritized his work because he knew how crucial it was to keep the train journey safe for passengers. Like my Grandpa and Nanna, taking days off or making an excuse to leave early from the work was never in my Dad's veins. He would say, "It's about taking responsibility and not running away from the work."

He was the man of Railways.

CHAPTER TWENTY-NINE

MINIMALISTIC BUSY LIFE

With great work comes great responsibility and a lot more busy hours. When Dad was promoted to Signal Engineer and was transferred to Daund, he had his own walky-talky. It was mandatory for S&T engineers to always keep it charged and handy. In case of emergency, he would receive a message on that walky-talky from an engineer on the field, so that he can immediately get to the emergency spot.

I loved that walky-talky. I was fascinated by hearing other people's voices on it. Whenever my sister and I would go to Dad's cabin to give him a lunch box, we would play with his walky-talky. Dad would even let us sit on his office chair and use his computer. We would draw something on the paint application.

One day, Aditi and I were waiting for Dad in his office. Mom had sent us to give him his lunch box. He was in the relay room and his walky-talky was on his desk. It started catching a signal and we heard someone speaking, "Mechanical failure at the point...." and the voice cut down.

"I think we should inform Dad," said my sister. I nodded. As we were heading towards the relay room in the basement, a loud siren started screeching in the train tracks.

Dad came out of the relay room. We handed him the walky-talky and told him about the message. The man from the other side repeated the message. Dad understood where he had to go and hurried out saying, "Wait in the cabin."

He hadn't even started with lunch. We obeyed his order and went back up to his office. We had nothing to do, so we powered on his computer to play a game, the one with the snake eating cubes and getting lengthier. Boring, but handy.

"What do you think has happened?" I asked Aditi.

"I am not sure, he said something about mechanical failure."

"What does that mean?"

"I don't know, it sounded serious though."

We were worried and wanted our father back with us. An hour passed but Dad didn't return. Soon, boredom consumed us, and now even computer games weren't interesting anymore. There was a landline phone in his office and we knew our home landline number. We called Mom and asked if we could come home. She said, "Keep the lunch box in the drawer of his desk and you can come home". Aditi kept a lunch box in the drawer, took out a small piece of paper, and wrote on it. "We are going home. Finish the lunch or Mom will scold you. See you at home :)" She kept the note on top of his lunch box and we went downstairs.

As we were walking by the tracks to get to Aditi's cycle, we saw a huge crowd. We were curious and decided to get a little closer to see what was going on. As we walked past the cabin, we saw a goods train had slid from the tracks. The engine was almost standing horizontal on the tracks and the rest of the carriages had slid to either side of the rail line. Fortunately, nothing bad happened to anyone. We saw all the engineers working in the field to solve the problem. We couldn't see Dad but decided to go home before he sees us hanging around railway tracks.

On our way to the parking lot, we spotted a huge crane, on its way to lift the goods train up and put it back on the tracks. But before that, it was important to find out why it slid down. When something like this happens, each department investigates the root cause of the accident and then decides the solution.

Dad and his team were searching for any crack or disarrangement in the tracks. Aditi and I already went home. We knew the chances of Dad finishing his lunch box were almost zero. It had happened so many times that he brought the tiffin back home; unfinished. He would eat that for dinner. Or sometimes, Mom had to throw it away because Dad was on the field for 36 hours or more.

There was a train track inspection trolley vehicle, which would run on the tracks to find any defects. The trolley vehicle did its work and found a crack half a mile away from the Daund station. It wasn't a big crack, but the track could not bear the pressure of a goods train and got dislocated. That's why the train slid down in the yard.

Usually, train tracks get serviced and replacement at particular intervals. In the case of minor cracks, a specific welding method works and the rail track becomes functional again. Dad had to stay there to make sure the welding process goes well.

When he returned home at midnight, Aditi and I were long asleep. The next morning though, we asked him about the incident.

"How did that train fall, Dad?" I asked and he told me about the cracks. Until then, I didn't know that those tracks could break or dislocate.

"You know that crushed stones around the rails? Those keep rails intact in one place. By the end of the day, those stones move away from the rails because of the vibration when the train passes. A team of people pushes those stones back in place, closer to the rails. In rare cases, rails get cracked and trains slid down."

Dad had seen so many horrible train incidents or people running in front of a fast train, he had seen worse of the worse. Back then, we were so young to understand how hard his job could be. How much he had to see, how much pressure he had to manage. It wasn't just a job. Millions of people travel by train, it was about their safety. People blindly trust trains for long route journeys, and Dad was one of the people behind the safe and happy travels of those people.

When we were complaining about waking up early to go to school, Dad was working endlessly by staying awake for hours and hours. And he did that with passion. He used to go to the office by cycle. His cycle trips between the office and home were uncountable. He never got tired. The engineers working above him or below him had bikes and cars. But Dad adored his cycle.

"Cycling is an exercise," he would say when I used to ask why he doesn't get a motorbike. He never wanted one. His life was minimal. He just had 3 pairs of office clothes, one pair of shoes, and a cycle. He never wore any perfume, nor did he have a fancy shaving kit. He was walking in the tracks on hot sunny days, sweating and thirsty. He never purchased anything costly for himself, but my sister and I had everything. That was his minimalistic busy life, dedicated to railways.

CHAPTER THIRTY

To the Next Station

Daund was a developed station in terms of the railways. As it was a Junction, the signals were electrical, the tracks had a double line, and six platforms for trains to arrive. When I was in elementary school, trains had evolved from the steam engine to the diesel engine. And Daund was getting ready for electric engines. Faster and reliable.

To make an electric engine run seamlessly, the Daund station had to adopt a new electrical infrastructure. Dad was on a team to create an environment for new engines. He was in charge of maintaining Route Relay Interlocking and developing a railway electrification system for Daund station. Basically, to make sure the relay room electric circuits communicate perfectly with the signals and tracks. Electrical equipment replaced the job of mechanical levers to set the tracks and crossings. The Station Master's office got upgraded with an advanced panel to set the tracks by pressing just a few buttons. The advanced panel has a map of tracks in the station, the color-coded LEDs to show the current status of all tracks, and the error detection mechanism is even better.

Dad had applied the same regulations at Daund that he did at Kedgaon to reduce the number of failures. From an average of 8 to 9 failures a month, he brought it to 1 or 2. To achieve all this, he worked endlessly, even on weekends. Inspection, footplates, and management would consume his time. Dad being home was very occasional. Sometimes, we didn't even get a chance to say hi. He would leave for work before Aditi and I woke up and would return when we were long asleep. We were getting used to the fact that Dad shows up randomly and leaves abruptly.

It was my Mom who managed the home and took care of her daughters. She was no less than Wonder Woman. She would clean our whole house every day including the front and back yard, the terrace, and the surrounding area. Maintaining the house was a time-consuming and tiring task. She took care of our house from her heart. Ladies from the neighbourhood would suggest that she should hire a gardener, but she enjoyed doing everything on her own.

Every morning, she would wake up at 4. Clean every corner of the house, then wash the clothes of every member in the house with her own hands. We didn't have a washing machine or dishwasher and neither did we have a maid to do it for us. Mom was against hiring a maid. She was particular in her work and would say, "Maids can never clean the house the way I want."

After laundry, she would pluck some flowers from the backyard garden for God's prayers and pooja. Then she would wake us up, and give us chocolate milk and breakfast. She then had a routine to prepare our lunch boxes and get us ready for school. By then, both my sister and I had our own cycles to go to school.

For the rest of the day, Mom would busy herself with chores. She was the busiest homemaker I knew. When Dad was working day and night for railways, Mom was doing the same at home.

It was Mom who attended all our PTA meetings back in school days. She would wait in line at a supermarket to buy groceries and vegetables. Mom even repaired broken mixers and DVD players. Not only that, she would clean the deep, large water tank up in the terrace, fix the broken terrace floor by applying cement, repair leakages in the house, and do regular servicing of the doors and gates of our home.

She was the man of the house. We have seen her do things that usually a man does. Heavy lifting and fixing stuff. She was well aware of what Dad had to do at his work. She did not want to bother him with problems at home. She learned to fix everything.

Her management skills were beyond our understanding. Aditi and I used to rely on her for so many things, including homework. She would stay up late with us in case we needed help with our studies. She never pushed both of her daughters about studies but created enough awareness that we would study regularly. As she had experience in teaching, some of my or Aditi's friends from the neighbourhood would occasionally come to our house. Mom would pause her work and sit with us to make sure we finish the homework. Without her teaching, my sister and I would have never been able to score good marks.

Mom didn't receive enough appreciation for what she was doing back then to hold the house together. Even Dad once said, "Without her, it would have been impossible for me to work. I blindly trust her with everything." Mom has been the finance minister of our home since always. Dad let her take care of budgeting, finances, and investments.

Mom and Dad together were living their own different lives to provide for their daughters. When Dad was standing on the field, with the hot sun bombarding heat and sweat, Mom was running constantly to our school, markets, and house to balance everything. They were a perfect match. I always wonder, if Dad had married someone else, she would have never been able to cope with Dad's work schedule. Mom was humble and self-sufficient. She never complained to Dad about why she should be the only one taking care of everything. "When you marry someone, you two become a team; the two wheels to keep the household running. One is incomplete without the other," she always says to us.

Dad had gained enough experience to be treated as an expert at his work. Under his supervision and maintenance, the Daund station got an award for the best management. He again won awards for his excellent work. Aditi and I were proud of our father and also thought the award belonged to both Mom and Dad.

I was in 5th grade when Dad was transferred to a different town. We all were having dinner together after so many days when Dad told us, "I have been transferred to Puntamba station as a Senior Signal Engineer."

"So, when are we leaving Dad?" I asked him.

"You, Aditi, and Mom will stay here. Only I am going," he replied. Aditi was old enough to understand Mom and Dad's decision. I was really mad at the central railways to send my father away. But he and Mom had decided that the kids and Mom will stay in the same town. It was for our school and routine. They didn't want us to suffer.

Dad was the one who had to suffer. He again had to be on his own in a town that was undeveloped. Before reporting to Puntamba town, Dad had to finish the upgraded training for 6 months at Secunderabad in South India. In a government job, it was very normal to get transferred. Grandpa had faced it and now Dad was experiencing it. Unlike Grandma, who went everywhere with Grandpa along with her kids, Mom was alone in Daund. Grandpa and Grandma would spend a few months of the year at each of their children's houses. Grandpa was obviously fond of Daund, but to spend quality time with his grandchildren, he would spend equal time with all of us.

The day arrived when Dad had to leave for Puntamba. Aditi and I helped him pack his bags. Mom prepared some snacks that he could use for at least a month. He was ready to go to the next destination of his work life.

"Okay then, I will see you soon," Dad said to both me and my sister. We wanted him to stay. But that wasn't possible. So we decided to come to terms with his busy life.

"Bye Dad, don't worry about the home," said Aditi who was now a mature girl. "Mom and I will manage the house and this creature too," she pointed at me. I frowned at her and made faces, but then focused on Dad, ignoring her comment.

"Bye, Dad. Bring new notebooks for me, would you?" I said. Dad always brought stationery from Mumbai or Secunderabad.

"Okay," he promised. "What else do you want?" he asked before leaving. I was in love with one of his journals with a logo of central railways. I had seen those journals and notepads on his desk. "I want a big notebook like yours."

He laughed, "You wanted that? You could have said it earlier. Alright though, I will get you one of those journals," he said before leaving.

Aditi and I waved at him and watched him drive away with his bag tied to the backseat of his cycle. Dad was on his way to the next station.

SUMMER VACATIONS IN PUNTAMBA

The engine whistle echoed around the town as the train arrived on the Puntamba platform in the middle of the night. Dad got off the train and sat on one of the benches near the ticket booking center. After a long 8 hours journey by passenger train on the hot summer day, the night breeze was peaceful. He sat there for a while, examining the surrounding. There were only two platforms facing each other. His office was adjacent to the main platform and the second platform seemed to be under re-construction. There was a lane of railway quarters behind both platforms.

Puntamba was a small village. After working with electrical signals at Kedgaon and Daund, the village brought my father back to mechanical signals. He stayed seated on the bench for a while before entering his new office. The night duty staff was working quietly.

He talked to the station master, shook hands with him, and went straight to his cabin. After having a quick tour of his office, Dad pulled out his journals and a few things required for work. Quickly, he wiped out the desk and chair to set it up for the next day. Now, the only problem was finding a place to spend the night. He hadn't got a railway quarter yet. Puntamba wasn't a city where one can find motels to live in. Besides, Dad was unaware of the town, and finding something in the middle of the night was not convenient. The only option left was the open waiting area on the platform.

The waiting area only had a couple of chairs. Dad pulled 2 chairs, placed them facing each other, and settled himself. Since his hostel days in Shahabad, Dad had always kept a pair of blankets and cotton sheets with him. He was tired and needed to get some rest. Quickly, he took out the blanket from his bag and pulled it over himself. Closing his eyes, Dad tried to get some sleep. To his surprise, he fell asleep quite quickly.

Dad had spent so many nights sleeping like this in the available waiting area. He had to travel a lot to different towns that he got used to this lifestyle. It wasn't a big deal for him. But for us, we felt like betraying him by sleeping on a cozy bed.

Dad was deep asleep when the morning shift crew reported to duty and night shift people went back home. His night went with barking dogs, chirping birds, and biting mosquitoes. Waking up with an aching body, he got up as one 7-AM train departed from the platform. Tucking the blanket back into the bag, Dad went to get fresh in a public toilet on the platform. As there was no place to take bath, he changed into a clean shirt and reported to duty at sharp 8 in the morning. After meeting the morning staff and introducing himself to Station Master, Dad got straight to work.

A knock on his office door brought his attention back from the open register in front of him. A man in his early 30s was standing outside the office.

"Good morning, sir," the man introduced himself, "I am Jaswant. I will be reporting to you from today." Dad called him in and offered to take a seat across the table.

As Dad was signing on the register, Jaswant was glancing at Dad's luggage. He saw Dad's blanket peeking out of the bag.

"Sir," Jaswant asked politely, "where did you spend the night, sir?"

Dad casually replied, closing the register, "In the waiting area. I didn't get a place to stay yet. So I made myself comfortable here." Soon a man came with a kettle of tea. He poured two cups and handed one to Dad, and the other to Jaswant.

"Sir, if I knew you had nowhere to go, I could have arranged something."

"It's alright Jaswant. I am sure I will figure something out," Dad replied. He was aware of the town's condition. He knew he was not going to get a place to live anytime soon. Dad had his tea in peace and asked Jaswant about the work in progress. Jaswant walked him through the status of work at the station and told him about the people working there.

My father spent some time getting to know his colleagues and guided them with a new set of work instructions.

When the staff went to resume their respective work, Jaswant reluctantly suggested, "Sir if you would like to get fresh, my room is just a block down the station."

"No no, that's alright. I will be fine."

"Sir, you won't find anything here."

Dad considered his offer wondering it would probably be better if he went with Jaswant. When they reached his room, Dad saw that Jaswant's house was neat and clean. It was a small room with a tiny counter in the corner for cooking. The quarter was well organized and tidy. There was a washroom at the back of the room with no hot water or tap water. Jaswant fetched a bucket of water from the tank nearby and placed it in the bathroom. Dad was used to taking a cold water bath. He had already forgotten basic luxuries, like hot water or a room to live in.

My father got fresh and wore a clean pair of ironed clothes. Jaswant had made coffee for both of them. Dad felt refreshed after that strong cup of coffee and gladly thanked Jaswant. Afterward, both of them went to work.

It was a bright summer day and Dad had a lot of work to do. To begin with, he asked Jaswant to get all the registers and reports for the past year. As Dad was going through the registers, he found a lot of problems. The reports were not thorough. The register didn't have all the details in some of the entries. It wasn't something he would expect from his staff. He wanted everything to be perfect.

"Call everyone you can for a meeting," Dad instructed Jaswant. He was disappointed after noticing the lack of discipline. In 15 minutes, everybody gathered in his office. He was seated with reports spread all over his desk. My father was famous for being strict. People in Puntamba have already heard how particular he was about work.

"Please be seated," Dad said gesturing towards the chairs arranged in his office. Everyone exchanged a quick nervous glance with one another and hesitated before taking a seat. Dad waited for them to settle down before he asked them about the reports.

"I have been reading the registers and reports of the past failures," Dad began talking. He asked about who wrote the report, why some entries were half missing, and why the reports weren't thorough. He had also checked the number of failures per month and that number was big. Now he knew why he had been transferred to Puntamba. The town needed discipline.

His team answered his questions. It wasn't on purpose, they said. They just did not see the need to be so disciplined in paperwork. That was not the way my father worked. So, he decided to set up strict rules. He explained how detailed he wanted the reports to be. Dad wanted his team to be on their best performance.

After the meeting, everybody got back to work. Dad received a call from his superiors asking about his first day. "It is going good so far," he replied. Dad spent the whole day understanding the most commonly occurring failures in the Puntamba to Manmad town rail line. He checked the relay room and talked to the cabin men. In a couple of hours, he had a tentative plan ready to execute in the town.

As lunchtime approached, the majority of the staff went home or opened their lunch boxes. Puntamba wasn't closer to Daund. Sending him a lunch box wasn't as easy as earlier. Dad took out some snacks from his bag and quickly ate his lunch in his cabin before resuming work. The day was going pretty much dull but he had a lot of work to do.

It was 6 in the evening when the office boy brought fresh tea. Dad had lost track of the time and needed to make an urgent call about his railway quarter. He dialed a number and asked about a place to live. Usually, every other department in railways gets allotted a certain number and type of railway quarters in the town as per the grade of employee. And S&T department comes under the essential category, so Dad was supposed to get the railway quarter.

"Sir, I am extremely sorry but currently, there isn't any quarter available. You have to wait for 2 months. The one opposite platform number 2 will be empty by then," said the man from the opposite side.

"2 months?" Dad was a bit disappointed to hear that. Now he was on his own in an unknown town without a place to stay. "So is there any guest house or at least a motel nearby?" he further asked.

"There are a few hostels in the main town. Around a 20-minute walk from the railway station."

"Okay, thanks." Dad hung up the phone and sat in his cabin, frustrated and tired. He decided to go see those hostels. Just as he was about to leave, Jaswant knocked on his office door.

"Are you leaving sir?" he asked my father, wondering if he got the place to stay.

"Umm? Yes," Dad replied, tidying his desk. "Do you know where the hostels are in the main town?"

Jaswant seemed worried. "Sir, those hostels are not good. The facilities are very uncomfortable. There is no proper water storage or clean functional washrooms. You are not planning to stay there, are you?" he asked with concern.

"I have no other option. The quarter will be available in 2 months."

Jaswant thought for a moment and generously offered a solution. "You can stay with me. It's just a matter of two months."

"What? No. I don't want to bother you," Dad replied almost immediately.

"Why would I be bothered, sir? We will be at work for most of our day. I will make sure you feel at home and stay comfortable."

Dad remained quiet. He really did not want to bother anyone. "Please, sir. Let me help you," Jaswant insisted and Dad thought it was probably better to stay with him.

Both of them went to Jaswant's quarter after work. Dad sat down at one of the chairs, still wondering if he should go check those hostels. Jaswant brought some water for his boss. He then emptied the majority of the cupboard for Dad and said, "You can unpack here if you would like." Jaswant was very helpful, but Dad did not want to take all of his space. He just arranged all his clothes in one compartment of the cupboard and put the bags on the loft.

"I will cook some dinner for us," said Jaswant. He turned on the kerosene burner and kept a pan on it. Dad was feeling uncomfortable, then thought this was his place for the next two months.

"I will help you," Dad got up from the chair enthusiastically. "I'll make Dal Tadka, it's my favorite dish. You will like it."

Both of them cooked dinner and enjoyed it in the front yard. All this time, Dad was not Jaswant's boss, he was his friend. But Jaswant was feeling awkward when his boss started helping him in the kitchen. "I won't live here if you won't let me help," Dad said to him. Jaswant finally nodded with a smile.

After dinner, Jaswant took my father to show around the town. It was different than Kedgaon, more of a village area. But the town was calm and steady. No chaos, no traffic. Pure air and chirping birds. After taking a long walk in the main town, away from the railway station, both of them returned home before bedtime. Jaswant only had a small single bed in his house.

"Sir, you sleep on the bed. I will sleep on the floor."

"Jaswant, you generously offered me a place to live. This is your house," Dad politely replied, "I am not your boss here. You take the bed, I have my sheets and blanket."

Dad spread his cotton sheet at the corner of the house and smiled at Jaswant, "I am fine. Good night."

From that day to the next two months, he stayed with Jaswant. Dad would clean the house, buy groceries, and help with cooking every time. Both of them would go to the office together. Everybody in the office knew that Dad was staying with Jaswant and thought why a senior officer did not get a railway quarter yet. Dad's team would invite him for lunch or dinner and he would go happily as a friend.

As a senior engineer, Dad had to travel from Puntamba to Nagar town to Manmad town for inspection. He was regularly arranging a round of servicing for all mechanical equipment. People around him started working with his rules and discipline. Soon enough, Dad observed improvements in all the reports. His staff was taking him seriously. The office felt like a lively place. All the inspections round were going smoothly under Dad's supervision.

Two months passed and Dad finally got a railway quarter. It was just behind the opposite platform. His office and the new quarter were literally in front of each other, separated by a pair of platforms and railway tracks. There was no solid fence, he could see his quarter from his office. Now he had a place to live.

"Jaswant, thanks a lot for everything," Dad said to the man who had helped him and became friends on the very first day. "I am inviting you to breakfast at my place tomorrow morning."

Jaswant smiled and agreed, "I will be there sir. It was nice having you here," he added. Dad collected all his belongings and went to his new railway quarter. The quarter was bigger than the one from kedgaon and more comfortable. Dad immediately had a thought, the quarter was big enough to call his family.

"This summer vacation, we are going to get some fresh village air," Mom announced. "Dad called us to stay with him at Puntamba." Aditi and I jumped with happiness.

~~

Usually, during the summer holidays, Mom, Aditi, and I would go to Nanna's house. Aunt Asha's daughters and uncle Avi's children would be there too. We would spend a week at Solapur, get pampered by Nanni, and return home with lots of snacks and gifts. But this summer holiday, we were going to Dad's new house.

Exactly at 11 in the morning, we boarded a train to Puntamba. As Puntamba was a small village, only passenger trains would stop at that town. Express trains would just pass by. We got inside the train, put our bags beneath the seat, and waited for the train to start. Back then, passenger trains had wooden seats. My sister and I would complain a lot. But Mom would say, "See, everyone around us is sitting comfortably. Just stay a bit patient."

The train started moving after 10 minutes and I pulled out my slate and chalk to play tick-tack-toe with my sister.

"Mom, when will we reach?" I asked as the train left Daund and headed towards Puntamba.

"It takes at least 5 hours to reach the town," Aditi replied focusing on the game we were playing.

"Okay."

We continued our little game. The view outside was beautiful. I saw farms, rivers, and little houses next to those farms. It was worth fighting with my sister to grab the window seat to myself. But of course, I had to switch the seat after every hour so that my sister can get to enjoy the window seat too.

I imagined walking into Dad's new office and finding a computer on his desk. We were going to stay there for more than a month, so I had made some plans.

The train kept stopping at every station, replacing our excitement with boredom. It was taking forever to take us to Dad. By 5 in the evening, we had reached only halfway.

"You said it takes only 5 hours." I snapped at my sister. "We should be there by now."

"Honey, the passenger train takes time. We will be there soon," replied my Mom. She was calm. I had never seen her bored or pissed.

"Okay," I rolled my eyes. I was annoyed and needed to get off that train as soon as I can. Mom had brought food for the three of us. She unpacked the tiffin and handed butter-Jam chapati rolls to us, and took one for herself. We ate our snacks, drank Kokum Serbat, and resumed our game. The train kept moving ahead, stopping at stations. Two more hours passed. How many hours to go, I wondered.

All of a sudden, the train stopped in the middle of two stations. It did not move for the next 20 minutes. We heard that the engine of our train had some technical issues.

"We will never reach," cried Aditi, now she was also annoyed. Mom took out a packet of cookies and handed it over to us. "Have some cookies you two," she said trying to help us pass some time.

Another half an hour passed and finally, we felt the familiar sudden jerk. The train was moving again, putting all of us in relief. Aditi and I were bored of playing the same game, so we started singing songs. I saw some more villages and watched the green farms from the window. Summer days were long, but the sun was setting already. Soon it was dark and I could not see the surroundings anymore. I asked my sister what time it was.

"It's 7," she replied. We boarded the train at 11 in the morning. How far was Dad living? Our train stopped again, just two stations behind Puntamba. It did not move too soon and I wondered how old the engine of the train was.

But to my surprise, the train started moving again after half an hour.

At almost 8 in the evening, we arrived at Puntamba station. I already spotted my Dad standing outside his office waiting for us. It was a long journey and I wanted to get home, eat dinner, and go to bed. We got off the train. Dad had a 'welcome to the town' smile on his face as he approached us.

"Let's get to the office first," he said. "I need to sign some papers. Then we will go home."

"Can I play on your computer?" I asked entering his office.

"There isn't one," he replied.

What? No computer? How was I supposed to draw the village farms and houses that I saw during the journey on the paint application? All my plans had ended before I even entered Dad's office. All of us sat in the available chairs across from Dad's desk. The office boy got some water for us. I glanced around when Dad was signing papers. The office was different. Nothing like Daund. It was smaller and kind of weird. Maybe because there was no computer for me to play with. I was disappointed but decided to cheer myself up.

We walked to Dad's new house by crossing the railway line to reach the opposite end of the tracks. It took us only 5 minutes to be there. The door facing the railway station was actually the back door. The front door was on the other side, but the back door was quickly reachable. There was a small porch behind the door where a car could fit easily. A porch had another door that opened into a living room. I saw the front door to the opposite wall. Dad turned on the lights by flicking the switch from an ancient switchboard and the whole house illuminated. It was kind of like a large box divided into 4 parallel parts. To the left of the living room was a kitchen, to the left of the kitchen was another small room, and to the extreme end was the bathroom. It was a really weird house, but it was good. Enough space for me to run and play.

"It's like a train carriage. Straight." A roar of laughter filled the room as I said it. Dad lifted me in his arms and gave me a hug.

We changed into our pajamas, had a quick dinner, and spread mattresses on the floor for all four of us to sleep. After fighting about who will sleep where; my sister and I slept comfortably and soon we were all snoring.

Sun rose and the room lit up with fresh sunlight. Mom was already up preparing Dad's lunch box. Aditi and I were still asleep. When sunlight hit our eyelids, we woke up, yawning and stretching our arms. There were red spots of mosquito bites all over our arms and legs.

Mom asked us to get ready soon as Dad was taking us to his office. There were no little kids in the neighbourhood. I knew I would be bored at home. It was better to be at Dad's office. We got ready, had milk and breakfast, and was waiting at the doorstep for Dad to come out.

"I am taking you on a ride," he said with a smile on his face. Mom waved at us from the door as we walked to Dad's office. He did some paperwork and took us out at the tracks.

"See that Push Trolley?" he pointed to a vehicle standing on one of the tracks. Aditi and I turned to see what it was. "That is a rail inspection vehicle. We are going to go on a ride on that trolley."

That vehicle was somewhat similar to an open minibus, with no roof. It was cute and I was excited to go on a ride. We sat on the bench over the trolley. The trolley-man was waiting for us to settle. "Ready?" he asked and I almost screamed, "Yes, ready."

The trolley started moving on the train track. Dad and the trolley-man were on duty. Aditi and I were having fun. We passed by our house and waved at Mom standing by the kitchen window.

We traveled about a mile from the station and back. And for the first time in my life, I saw mechanical signals. I found those arm signals very interesting. Dad explained how those signals work and for the next few days, that was my game. To check the signal hand angle from the window and wait for the train.

When we arrived at the station, Dad took us to his cabin. "This is for both of you," he said handing over two empty journals. There was a central railway symbol on it. Dad had kept my wish in mind. I jumped in happiness and hugged him, "Thanks Dad. You are the best". I had brought coloring pens and now my life was sorted. Uncle Jaswant dropped both of us back home.

It was a wonderful morning and I was looking forward to the rest of the day. After lunch, I decided to spend some time doodling on the new notebook. Aditi rather preferred to write some essays.

In the evening, Dad came home early and took us out to dinner. We walked to the main town. On the way, I saw beautiful houses with roof tiles and wooden fences. In the main market, a couple in their late 40s had a *Dhaba* (Small diner). It was crowded and somewhat messy. But as soon as we entered the *Dhaba*, the delicious smell made my stomach growl. Dad chose a corner table and ordered 4 Thali. There was a small TV hung on the opposite wall telecasting a game of cricket. People were cheering and shouting.

Soon, a lady placed 4 plates on our table, smiling ear to ear. "Enjoy the meal," she said and got back to the kitchen. On the plate I saw, a mixed vegetable sabji, 2 Rotis, roasted papad, steamed rice, pickle, and a sweet dish. The fragrance of that spicy sabji was amazing. "Dig in," Dad said and we were all lost in the food for the next 20 minutes. For a change, I finished the plate. It was deliciously spicy food. I would never forget that place.

"You like it?" asked Mom, shocked to see my empty plate.

"Very much," I replied hoping Dad would bring us here more often.

Dad paid the bill and tipped the cook as his little daughter had finished the dinner. We walked back home. Dad was happy to be with his family after a long time.

The next day, we went on a small picnic at the Godavari River in the town. The temple at the river bank was beautiful and peaceful. While Mom and Dad were sitting on the stairs of a temple, Aditi and I ran along the river bank to put paper boats into the water.

The holidays were indeed going really fun. On weekends, if Dad had some time off from work, we would go to the nearest town for shopping. Sometimes, in the evening, we would go out to buy groceries or to meet Dad's friends. Jaswant uncle would come to play with us or we would go to his place for snacks.

The summer vacation at Puntamba was one of the best and most memorable vacations of my life.

CHAPTER THIRTY-TWO

TRAINS WERE MY FAMILY

Every year, my sister and I would look forward to finishing the exams and planning the vacation. Dad was in Puntamba for about three years. Earlier, we would at least see him four times a week, but when he moved to Puntamba, not even a glimpse of him. During those years, we would spend the summer holidays with him, which meant we would see him once a year. Dad missed every festival. We enjoyed the lights of Diwali when Dad was alone in Puntamba without electricity in his house.

Aditi and my school days went without his presence for our annual function where we won prizes. He never had a chance to see both of his daughters performing in school events and winning awards. Mom was always there. She attended every event at our school. People would come to her and say, "Your daughters are gems." She would feel proud and wish Dad was there to see all that.

Dad turned the workflow at Puntamba upside down. Not just discipline but proper work awareness. No matter how many nights he had to spend sleepless, he admired his work. "Once you start something, you finish it." he would say to us. His enthusiasm always made me wonder if I will ever be able to dedicate myself to my job to this extent. Aditi and I are Dad's daughters, of course, we love our work. Dad taught us how to surrender to the job and enjoy every moment of it, and Mom taught us how to be patient in every situation.

After three years in Puntamba, Dad won another Chief Signalling and Telecommunication award and was transferred back to Daund. We all were happy that Dad was finally going to be home, or at least in the same town. Now he had his own mobile phone which would ring millions of times a day calling him to work. Sometimes, we would even feel the illusion of his phone ringing. The ringtone was stuck in our heads. Whenever his phone rang, Dad would get dressed and go to work on his cycle. "Why don't you switch it off for a few hours, Dad? To get some sleep?" I once asked.

"That's running away from responsibilities. Besides, I wouldn't like it if I couldn't reach the emergency spot and something terrible happened. I will always run for the train's safety," he replied.

Good thing was, we were able to reach him on his phone. Mom would call him to ask at which station he was working to send the lunch box by train. If he ever had an emergency, he would call and inform us that he would be late. Late meant anything, late at night or after two days. There was no way to predict when he will return home. We stopped asking eventually. He would show up at home randomly. He was there, but not really.

Often, people would ask me and my sister, "Why your father never attends any function?" I wished I could explain what my Dad's work really was. How much busy he had been for years.

Sometimes, our own relatives thought that Dad was lying about work because he did not want to engage in family functions. That was not true and I hated people for assuming that. The man had no time to eat. Mom would say, "We do not owe an explanation about Dad's work to anyone. Just say he is busy, okay?" And that's what we did.

In the year 2007, Dad started having enormous Knee pain. He couldn't even walk properly. Walking in tracks was a part of his duty that came with the price of the knee trouble. He didn't show it but we could see how much pain he was in. Grandpa insisted on seeing a doctor in Pune city. The doctor prescribed some painkillers and instructed knee exercises. It took him more than a year to recover. He did not stop working even during his treatment. He went to work every day, rode his cycle despite having pain, and walked in the tracks even when it was hard to stand. For him, work always came first. Eventually, he beat the knee pain and was healthy again. There wasn't a thing that could stop my father from serving central railways.

Days passed. Years passed. And we grew up watching our Dad being enthusiastic and a workaholic. The man was now 50 years old but was still as fit as a flea. He still traveled by cycle and still lived a minimalistic life. He still worked day and night without getting tired. And his daughters wondered how does he do that? We would get tired after an extra hour of class and Dad was still running.

Meanwhile, Aditi completed her engineering degree from Pune, got a good job, and married a man she fell in love with. Her married life and my college life were going amazing in the city we both adored; Pune.

In 2014, Dad was one of the best employees in the Daund section. He got promoted to the position of Chief Signal Inspector. The same post where Grandpa once worked. We all were very proud of Dad's achievements. If Grandpa was alive, he would have cried in happiness. He would have been a proud father.

Dad now had a big office in Daund and a section assigned where he had to make 12 inspections per month, including surprise and night inspections. Apart from signal inspection, he was also in charge of inspecting the insides of trains such as the engine, working of all safety equipment, break/guard van, and crew lobby. He would travel by engine for footplate inspection, which involved checking the visibility of signals from the engine and the equipment inside the engine to ensure proper functioning. Then again, he had to check recent medical reports of the crew to make sure they are fit to drive the train. He has some great stories to share from those inspections.

Dad's office was surrounded by fences and unevenly grown trees. The office building was made up of stone walls from the British era and had three office spaces in total. Dad decided to give that building a fancy makeover. First thing, he hired people to properly trim the trees and fix broken fences. Then he decided to make a small temple in the garden area. To make the sitting area outside the office building more comfortable, he built shades and benches. Within two months, his office turned into a beautiful workplace.

Dad's office staff admired him for redecorating the workspace and improving the sitting arrangement of the staff. When the temple and garden were ready, Mom received an invitation from Dad's office staff for the first Pooja. She wore her favorite saree and went to Dad's office. Mom and Dad did the honor of the first Pooja and circulated Laddus as *Prashad*.

In those days, Dad also had his own office car with 'Government Vehicle, Central Railways,' written on it. Yet, he used that vehicle only to travel for work out of town. Otherwise, he adored his cycle. "Cycle keeps me healthy and down to earth," he would say. Whenever I was leaving for the morning train to Pune, I would insist he let me drop him at work.

My college life was fun, accompanied by trains. I didn't like the college hostel and preferred to run home every now and then. It was super exciting. Being a daughter of a central railway officer, I had a student railway pass with access to any train running between Pune and Daund. I experienced that thrill of rushing to the station, boarding a train to go to college, and again rushing to get the train back home. During exams, Dad would make some calls to let me know which train was available for me to reach college on time. I would travel by a 5 AM train and return by a 7 PM train after exams. It was a hectic schedule. But I didn't care as long as I was coming home every day. Even my sister preferred staying home and traveling by train to work. Basically, in my family, everyone had a 'Train life'. Nobody wanted to leave Daund.

My Engineering degree and Dad's last 4 years of work-life were going parallelly. Four years passed so quickly. In the year 2018, I graduated from college and Dad was retiring from work in a week.

"You have to give a speech," Dad said to me as I was planning his retirement party, "I was never there to listen to your speeches in your school's annual programs. This is my chance."

"Of course Dad. How could I not," I replied, making a list of guests.

Aditi, my sister was a mother now. My little nephew Anay, our little toddler, and the world's cutest baby boy, was playing with a toy car with his Grandpa.

"What are you going to wear?" I asked my sister who was feeding an apple to her little son.

"Indowestern gown, the one I wore on Diwali."

"Really? I am going to wear that red dress I stole from you." I giggled. She glared at me and shook her head.

Party planning was fun. Dad was making calls to invite people. The ceremony was planned in the same library hall where my Mom and Dad got engaged. In about a week, Dad was going to walk away from trains.

Trains were an integral part of my family, Trains were my family.

CHAPTER THIRTY-THREE

THE FAREWELL

It's not about how you live your life, it's about what you achieve in life. Small or big. But if it made a change in your or someone else's life, you did a great job. My Dad decided to work for Central Railways and achieved great success. For me and my sister, he is our hero.

On the day of Dad's farewell, our whole house was filled with guests. My uncles, aunts, and cousins were all there to attend the party, to celebrate his work life. We all got ready and went to Dad's office for the last time. Behind his desk, there was a wooden board with the names of all the Chief Signal Inspectors who ever sat and worked in that office. The very first name was my Grandpa's Mr. Ranganath Yeshwant Pantoji. And the very recent name was my Dad's Mr. Anand Rangnath Pantoji. My chest filled with pride when I glanced at that board.

I asked Dad to take a seat and have a moment alone in his office. Teardrops rolled down the corner of his eyes when he was glancing around the place where he had spent countless hours. Aditi asked him to smile and clicked a few photographs to cherish a memory forever. Dad spent a good 15 minutes in his office before bidding goodbye to that wonderful place.

~~

Almost every member of the Daund railway section and Solapur Division was attending Dad's farewell. Dad also invited uncle Sameer, his best friend from Shahabad. Mr. Gokhale, Mr. and Mrs. Patil from Kedgaon were also there with their children and grandchildren. Jaswant and Dad's Puntamba team were glad to meet him again. Everyone was there, Dad's family, along with his work family.

The venue, wide-open ground in front of the library hall, was welcoming people from the Central Railways. The stage was decorated with flowers and lights. A long table and a few chairs were arranged for the committee members to sit along with my father. A long red carpet from the entrance of the venue to the stage was adding more beauty to the party. And, a poster behind the stage was displaying in the big bold letters: 'Farewell Party for Chief Signal Inspector Mr. Anand Pantoji.' All the arrangements were made by Dad's office staff. One of his colleagues was on the stage to host the program. He announced Dad's name and asked him to take a seat on the stage. Dad was sitting on a middle chair behind the table with mom sitting beside him with pride. She was shy to be on the stage but proud at the same time

Dad's closest friend came up to the stage and talked about him. Some shared their experience with my father and how he taught them discipline. Some praised his fitness and some applauded him for his finest achievements. And then, my name was called for the speech. I hadn't prepared anything but I knew exactly what I wanted to say.

I walked up on the stage and took a mic. I looked at Dad who was already smiling at me. Out of all the speeches, he was waiting for mine.

"Thank you all for being here to celebrate my Dad's 34 years of glorious work life. It wasn't long ago when I said to Dad that we all should go on a little family trip. I was waiting for him to get a little break and stay with us. But when I saw him sitting in his office an hour ago, I understood how much he will miss this place. Dad had worked so hard, with dedication and discipline. He had been and always will be an inspiration to me and my sister. We grew up watching him rush to the office at any time of the day or night. He dedicated his life to railways. And he never abandoned his cycle. I think that's a part of his identity. Our little trips to Puntamba, the engine ride, and each train experience will always be memorable.

In all these years, things changed a lot. But one thing still hasn't changed. Dad still never purchases a pair of shoes for himself without my opinion. That's kind of our thing and I promise you, Dad, that this will never change. I will never change and neither will Aditi. We are still your little daughters who are very much proud of you. And Mom, I think we never said it to you, but you are awesome. Without you, Dad wouldn't have been able to work. You looked after the home and your daughters. You did not get enough appreciation. But today I want to say, you worked as hard as Dad and I am proud of you both. I don't know if Aditi and I will ever be able to be like you. Mom and Dad, you did everything you could to give us a comfortable life and I am thanking you for that. Aditi and I are lucky to be your daughters." I ended my speech and a rhythmic applause rose in the audience. I could see tears in Mom's and Dad's eyes, but they were broadly smiling at me. Before stepping down the stage, I hugged my parents. Grandma was sitting in the front row. She called me closer and kissed me on the cheek. I wished Grandpa was there too.

After my speech, Dad talked about his experience and the amazing people he had worked with. He shared some of the craziest incidents and some really emotional ones. His teammates brought him loads of gifts and bouquets.

Aditi and I made sure everybody had lunch and enjoyed the sweet dishes. Dad and our family members were last to have lunch. We sat in a big circle to have a meal together. We talked about so many things, Grandpa's memories and our childhood. Dad was feeling the warmth of his family. The man had dedicated his life to something that now was slipping away. He wanted to travel back in time to have some more time with trains and his work. I knew it would be hard for him to leave everything behind. But now was the time for us to keep him busy with family time.

That day I saw how many people were grateful for my father's guidance.

Dad indeed had a glorious career.

CHAPTER THIRTY-FOUR

EPILOGUE: TRAINS COULDN'T LEAVE HIM

"Let's go to the dinner tonight," suggested my sister as we were all sitting together to enjoy the Sunday evening. I was playing peek-a-boo with my little nephew Anay. Mom was, as usual, cleaning something in the kitchen and Dad was reading a newspaper in the balcony of our new flat in Pune city. We still go to Daund. But Pune is our new home where both my sister and I have our jobs.

"Of course, let's go. Where do you suggest?" I asked her and she suggested a new restaurant nearby. It had been two months since Dad's retirement. We were happy to see him home all the time. Mom finally had a chance to spend some quality time with her husband. We all got ready and booked a cab to the restaurant. Little Anay was saying something in his own baby-language with my Mom.

The ambiance of the restaurant was beautiful and family-friendly, just the way my parents prefer. Placing the order, we were chatting about Anay's new daycare. He was peacefully sitting in Aditi's lap speaking a few words that he learned from his daycare.

As we were waiting for our food, Dad's phone rang. There was a time when he would receive a call every 5 minutes. After retirement, his phone occasionally rang.

"Maybe I should take this," he said and went out of the restaurant seeking some silence. When he came back, he seemed a little distracted. A pinch of excitement and confusion was visible on his face.

"What is it?" I curiously asked.

"I have got a job offer," he announced.

And now as I am writing this book, a private organization hired my father as an expert in the electrification of trains in the Daund-Baramati section. The company was searching for people with good experience in that field and came across Dad's profile. They decided to offer him a job. He has been developing a route of electric engines for local trains to run between those two stations.

It's been more than two years and Dad is still working at his new job after retirement. A part of me thought he needed a break from work life. But a part of me knew he would never be able to get away from that life. "One should always stay active. It gives a purpose to your life ahead," Dad always says. Fortunately, his new job is 9 to 5 and a little less hectic. He spends a good amount of time with his family and goes to work every day.

I remember how emotional he was on the day of his farewell. That day, he left the trains...

But trains couldn't leave him.

—

Enjoyed the train journey? Support my Indie Author Journey by leaving a rating and review on Amazon and Goodreads. It would mean the world to me.

Subscribe to my <u>newsletter</u> to receive updates about my books.

Say Hi to me on Social Media: @ruchapantoji

About The Author

Rucha Pantoji is the author of 'Dreaming Among The Pages' and 'What Does Your Dad Do?'

She started writing stories when she was in school, hoping one day she would publish her book. But as she grew up, destiny brought her into an Engineering College and she briefly pretended to have her life together by taking a (pretty boring) tech job.

After hating her job and complaining about it every damn day, she finally decided to write stories rather than lines of codes.

Now she spends her day writing stories and night curled up in a bed with a book until her eyes burn. Brewing a refreshing Chai is her hobby apart from collecting cute stationery and handbags.

Find Out More About Rucha:

https://www.ruchapantoji.com/

Also By Rucha Pantoji

Dreaming Among The Pages

www.ruchapantoji.com

Note From The Author

Dear Reader,

Thanks a lot for reading 'What Does Your Dad Do?'. If any of the incidents put a smile on your face, I'd be beyond happy.

I always like to connect with readers and fellow writers. Feel free to contact me if you have anything to share with me. I would love to know what you are working on.

I tried my best to avoid typos. However, sometimes, mistakes do slip through unintentionally. If you found any mistakes, please email me at hello@ruchapantoji.com or message me on Instagram.

Once again, thank you for reading my book :)

www.ingramcontent.com/pod-product-compliance
Lightning Source LLC
Chambersburg PA
CBHW071512140726
47997CB00005B/1943